New Directions for
Institutional Research

Paul D. Umbach
EDITOR-IN-CHIEF

J. Fredericks Volkwein
ASSOCIATE EDITOR

Using Mixed-Methods Approaches to Study Intersectionality in Higher Education

Kimberly A. Griffin
Samuel D. Museus
EDITORS

Number 151 • Fall 2011
Jossey-Bass
San Francisco

USING MIXED-METHODS APPROACHES TO STUDY INTERSECTIONALITY IN
HIGHER EDUCATION
Kimberly A. Griffin and Samuel D. Museus (eds.)
New Directions for Institutional Research, no. 151
Paul D. Umbach, Editor-in-Chief

NEW DIRECTIONS FOR INSTITUTIONAL RESEARCH (ISSN 0271-0579, electronic
ISSN 1536-075X) is part of The Jossey-Bass Higher and Adult Education
Series and is published quarterly by Wiley Subscription Services, Inc., A
Wiley Company, at Jossey-Bass, 989 Market Street, San Francisco, California 94103-1741 (publication number USPS 098-830). Periodicals
Postage Paid at San Francisco, California, and at additional mailing
offices. POSTMASTER: Send address changes to New Directions for Institutional Research, Jossey-Bass, 989 Market Street, San Francisco, California 94103-1741.

SUBSCRIPTIONS cost $109 for individuals and $297 for institutions, agencies, and libraries in the United States. See order form at end of book.

EDITORIAL CORRESPONDENCE should be sent to Paul D. Umbach, Leadership, Policy and Adult and Higher Education, North Carolina State University, Poe 300, Box 7801, Raleigh, NC 27695-7801.

New Directions for Institutional Research is indexed in Academic Search
(EBSCO), Academic Search Elite (EBSCO), Academic Search Premier
(EBSCO), CIJE: Current Index to Journals in Education (ERIC), Contents
Pages in Education (T&F), EBSCO Professional Development Collection
(EBSCO), Educational Research Abstracts Online (T&F), ERIC Database
(Education Resources Information Center), Higher Education Abstracts
(Claremont Graduate University), Multicultural Education Abstracts
(T&F), Sociology of Education Abstracts (T&F).

Microfilm copies of issues and chapters are available in 16mm and 35mm,
as well as microfiche in 105mm, through University Microfilms, Inc., 300
North Zeeb Road, Ann Arbor, Michigan 48106-1346.

www.josseybass.com

THE ASSOCIATION FOR INSTITUTIONAL RESEARCH was created in 1966 to benefit, assist, and advance research leading to improved understanding, planning, and operation of institutions of higher education. Publication policy is set by its Publications Committee.

For information about the Association for Institutional Research, write to the following address:

AIR Executive Office
1435 E. Piedmont Drive
Suite 211
Tallahassee, FL 32308-7955

(850) 385-4155

air@mailer.fsu.edu
http://airweb.org

CONTENTS

EDITORS' NOTES

There is a famous Indian legend in which six blind men feel different parts of an elephant and draw conclusions about what they are touching. In the story, one man touches the elephant's side and concludes that the elephant is like a wall. A second man touches the elephant's tusk and infers that the animal is shaped like a spear. A third man touches the elephant's trunk and concludes that the elephant is shaped like a snake. A fourth man touches the elephant's knee and asserts that the animal is shaped like a tree. The fifth and sixth men touch the elephant's ear and tail and conclude that the elephant is shaped like a fan and a rope, respectively. All six men are certain that they are correct and argue with each other. They are partially right, but they are all completely wrong (Saxe, 1963).

In some ways, this tale is analogous to the quantitative-qualitative paradigm wars. Researchers have argued for decades about the validity, utility, and desirability of quantitative and qualitative methods. In the legend of the blind men and the elephant, incorporation of all six individual perspectives could have resulted in a holistic understanding of the nature of the elephant. Similarly, although quantitative and qualitative researchers have historically debated about quantitative and qualitative methods, it is increasingly acknowledged that each approach contributes a valuable perspective to research that can lead to more holistic understandings of various phenomena (Johnson, Onwuegbuzie, and Turner, 2007). Accordingly, there is a growing recognition of the value of mixed-methods approaches. Indeed, as we discuss in Chapter Two of this volume, the last two decades have, by and large, been defined by the emergence of paradigmatic pragmatism—the methodological paradigm based on the philosophical perspective that positivist-oriented quantitative methods and constructivist-oriented qualitative techniques are complimentary rather than oppositional.

Despite the growth of paradigmatic pragmatism in higher education, there are still instances in which researchers are discouraged or receive signals that they are second-class because their quantitative methods are not comprehensible or their qualitative findings are not generalizable. As paradigmatic pragmatists, we both use quantitative, qualitative, and mixed-methods research in our own scholarship, selecting the methods that can most effectively address the questions we seek to answer. We believe that it is no longer acceptable to spend valuable time and resources arguing about the validity or desirability of quantitative or qualitative methods; nor is it suitable to view quantitative or qualitative methods as inadequate. In this volume, we aim to demonstrate not only that quantitative and qualitative methods are *both* useful but also that they can be complementary tools for understanding important individuals, groups, processes, and phenomena on college and university campuses.

Ten years ago, Borland (2001) and his colleagues made the case that mixed-method approaches are useful tools for conducting institutional research and assessment. The contributors of this volume build on their work, applying mixed-methods research to engagement in intersectional analyses in higher education—examination of how multiple identities shape the experiences of individuals and groups in postsecondary education. Our personal experiences and commitment to our respective social justice agendas warrant a greater focus on intersectionality in higher education research and discourse. Regarding the former, we understand that our multiple identities have shaped our own experiences in unique and complex ways. Regarding the latter, in many ways intersectionality research is in its infancy in the field of higher education. In addition, we believe it holds great promise for advancing knowledge in higher education, as well as the ability of institutions and institutional researchers to understand and most effectively serve their students and faculty.

This volume offers institutional researchers several examples of the ways in which quantitative and qualitative methods can be integrated for a better grasp of how members of our educational communities understand and experience their environments on the basis of their multiple identities. The first two chapters provide the context for this volume. In Chapter One, we define intersectionality and discuss the importance of incorporating intersectional analysis into scholarly and institutional research, encouraging researchers to move beyond models and analytic strategies that focus solely on a singular aspect of student identity. In Chapter Two, we give an overview of the epistemological underpinnings of mixed methodology, discuss key considerations in designing a mixed-methods study, present a useful typology of mixed-methods research designs, and describe ways to overcome the challenges associated with conducting mixed-methods research.

In the subsequent chapters, invited authors illustrate the multiple ways in which qualitative and quantitative methods can be integrated to understand the complexity of identity and experiences of marginalized groups in the academy. Chapters Three and Four focus on faculty members. In Chapter Three, Meghan Pifer illustrates how to integrate social network analysis with interviews to explore how faculty make choices about the frequency and nature of their interactions with their colleagues according to the multiple aspects of their identities. In doing so, she illuminates how perceived similarities and differences shape faculty members' access to information and resources that are important to faculty development, satisfaction, and success. In Chapter Four, Kimberly Griffin, Jessica Bennett, and Jessica Harris demonstrate how qualitative interviews can illuminate nuances in individual and group experiences that are not fully captured in examinations of large-scale quantitative surveys. They illustrate this reality using the example of a study that focuses on how black male and female faculty members engage in service, believe their work is evaluated, describe how faculty colleagues perceive them, and evaluate their stress as a result of these experiences.

The remaining four chapters focus on students' experiences. In Chapter Five, Samuel Museus shows how to integrate the analysis of a national quantitative dataset with qualitative interviews to explore college access among first-generation Asian Americans and Pacific Islanders. In doing so, he demonstrates how the voices of students can explain the causes of inequities identified in national quantitative datasets. In Chapter Six, Nolan Cabrera presents an analysis of racial ideology of white males to illustrate how researchers can use qualitative interview data to drive an analysis of a quantitative longitudinal dataset. Dina Maramba and Samuel Museus then demonstrate in Chapter Seven how quantitative and qualitative data can be analyzed concurrently in research and assessment to generate a more accurate understanding of how race and gender shape students' experiences within the campus climate and sense of belonging.

In our final chapter, Casandra Harper uses the findings of a mixed-methods inquiry to challenge current conceptions about racial categorization and practices for gathering institutional data on students' identity. She problematizes surveys that ask students to "check the box" or even "check multiple boxes," arguing that these questions can be troublesome for students who embrace multiple racial/ethnic identities and do not reflect the shifting nature of identity, and she makes multiple recommendations to better assess the racial/ethnic representation in one's institutional community, highlighting the importance of multiple measures of identity.

Kimberly A. Griffin
Samuel D. Museus
Editors

References

Borland, K. W., Jr. "Qualitative and Quantitative Research: A Complimentary Balance." In K. W. Borland Jr. (ed.), *Balancing Qualitative and Quantitative Information for Effective Decision Support*. New Directions for Institutional Research, no. 112. San Francisco: Jossey-Bass, 2001.

Johnson, R. B., Onwuegbuzie, A. J., and Turner, L. A. "Toward a Definition of Mixed-Methods Research." *Journal of Mixed-Methods Research*, 2007, 1(2), 112–133.

Saxe, J. G. *The Blind Men and the Elephant: John Godfrey Saxe's Version of the Famous Indian Legend*. New York: Whittlesey House, 1963.

KIMBERLY A. GRIFFIN *is an assistant professor of education policy studies at the Pennsylvania State University and a research associate in the Center for the Study of Higher Education.*

SAMUEL D. MUSEUS *is an assistant professor of educational administration at the University of Hawai'i Manoa.*

NEW DIRECTIONS FOR INSTITUTIONAL RESEARCH • DOI: 10.1002/ir

1

In this chapter, the authors discuss how understandings of individuals and groups in higher education research are limited by overreliance on one-dimensional analyses. They also underscore the importance of intersectionality research as one method to address such limitations.

Mapping the Margins in Higher Education: On the Promise of Intersectionality Frameworks in Research and Discourse

Samuel D. Museus, Kimberly A. Griffin

Both qualitative and quantitative research that categorizes students along singular dimensions of identity provide limited information, which can restrict the ability of higher education scholars and institutional researchers to fully—and sometimes accurately—understand and respond to problems that exist in postsecondary education. Consider these two scenarios:

A faculty member is troubled by the disproportionately high number of Asian American students leaving and failing his classes, so he requests data on this group from his campus's institutional research office. The following week, the office sends him a statistical report, which indicates that Asian Americans have grade point averages, a persistence rate, and a graduation rate higher than all other racial groups on campus. The faculty member concludes that his observations must not be representative of the population from which his students come and ceases his investigation.

During a qualitative climate assessment at an institution at which black students constitute more than 50 percent of the student body, a researcher interviews a first-year black male college student. The student tells the researcher that he cannot find other people like him on campus and is thinking about dropping out. The researcher probes with questions about why the interviewee feels this way but is unable to uncover the reasons behind those feelings. Given that the other black participants in the climate

New Directions for Institutional Research, no. 151, Fall 2011 © Wiley Periodicals, Inc.
Published online in Wiley Online Library (wileyonlinelibrary.com) • DOI: 10.1002/ir.395

assessment did not report a similar problem, the researcher concludes that this student is an outlier and his statements do not require further inquiry.

There are differences in these two scenarios. In the first example, the institutional research office analyzed quantitative institutional data, while the researcher in the second scenario conducted an interview for a qualitative campus climate assessment. However, the examples also have much in common. First, in both cases researchers relied on the socially constructed and commonly used concepts of race and racial categories to label students, investigate student-related problems, analyze student data, and interpret their findings. Second, as a result of this unquestioned reliance on data disaggregated or understood through the lens of race and racial categories, individuals in both examples had questions that went unanswered. Finally, and perhaps most problematic, the students' problems in these two scenarios went misunderstood and unaddressed.

If the researchers in these two scenarios had thought about the multiple aspects of their students' identities when conducting their inquiries, they might have asked different questions and generated different conclusions. What if, in the first scenario, the students who take courses in the faculty member's department were disproportionately low-income Cambodian refugee students who were the first in their family to attend college, and the institutional research office analyzed data primarily made up of a large number of affluent third-generation Asian Indian and Korean American undergraduates? And what if the student in the second scenario was a gay black male who could not find a safe and supportive environment on campus in which he could comfortably express both his black and gay identities? In these cases, researchers exploring the intersections between race and ethnicity or race and sexual orientation might engage in more critical analyses of their data and generate more accurate conclusions about their students' experiences and the larger issues that exist on their respective campuses.

Delineating and Defining the Types of Intersectionality

In her important work on intersectionality, Kimberé Crenshaw (1991) discussed identity politics and asserted that "the problem with identity politics is not that it fails to transcend difference, as some critics charge, but rather the opposite—that it frequently conflates or ignores intra-group differences" (p. 1241). She also discussed how such conflation is problematic because it fails to capture the ways in which multiple social identities shape the lives of oppressed individuals.

Since Crenshaw's illumination of the utility of intersectionality perspectives, scholars have argued that there is a unique experience at the intersection of individuals' identities, and efforts to isolate the influence of any one social identity fails to capture how membership in multiple identity groups can affect how people are perceived, are treated, and experience college and university environments (Berger and Guidroz, 2009; Crenshaw, 1989, 1991). This reality sets the foundation for the current chapter, which is focused on discussing the problematic conflation of intragroup differences in higher education research and discourse and the role of intersectionality in addressing that problem.

Before moving forward with our discussion, a few definitions are warranted. *Intersectionality* can be defined as the "relationships among multiple social dimensions and modalities of social relations and subject formations" (McCall, 2005, p. 1771). In simpler terms, it can be defined as the processes through which multiple social identities converge and ultimately shape individual and group experiences (Shields, 2008). *Structural intersectionality* refers to how multiple social systems intersect to shape the experiences of, and sometimes oppress, individuals (Crenshaw, 1991). In higher education, for example, structural intersectionality can be used to make sense of how both racial and gender inequities converge to shape the experiences of women of color in higher education. *Political intersectionality* refers to how the multiple social groups to which an individual belongs pursue different political agendas, which can function to silence the voices of those who are at the intersection of those social groups (Crenshaw, 1991). For example, political intersectionality would explain a case in which racial minority students refuse to address discrimination against lesbian, gay, bisexual, and transgender (LGBT) students of color to avoid having those issues become public and risking tainting the image of those communities of color. Finally, when we use the terms *intersectionality research*, *intersectionality framework*, or *intersectional analysis*, we are referring to the utilization of intersectionality to approach and conduct empirical social science research. In the following sections, we discuss how higher education researchers can use intersectionality and intersectional analyses to develop more informed understandings of the experiences of students, as well as faculty, administrators, and staff in higher education.

Intersectionality as an Integrative Concept

Although higher education researchers may often compare the experiences of men with those of women, heterosexuals with those of LGBT individuals, or white and racial minority groups, such comparisons are limited in their ability to illuminate individuals' and groups' unique experiences accurately or holistically. In reality, when asked "Who are you?" most students, faculty, and administrators in higher education would not respond with a single identity. Rather, an individual's sense of self can be based on many groups with which he or she identifies, and people can be defined simultaneously by their race, ethnicity, class, gender, sexuality, religion, and other aspects of their identities (Jones, 2009).

NEW DIRECTIONS FOR INSTITUTIONAL RESEARCH • DOI: 10.1002/ir

In response to the limitations of focusing on a singular social identity in understanding individual experiences, researchers in some academic fields are paying attention to intersectionality (e.g., Choo and Ferree, 2010; Shields, 2008). Indeed, a growing number of scholars, particularly in women's studies and critical race theory (CRT), have used principles of intersectionality in their analyses (Berger and Guidroz, 2009). Those employing intersectional analyses strive to understand the unique ways in which multiple intersecting social identities come together to shape one's experiences, making distinctions in how individuals experience and engage their environments as a result of their unique position at particular intersections, rather than focusing attention on a singular identity (e.g., Choo and Ferree, 2010; McCall, 2005; Ramachandran, 2005; Shields, 2008).

Women's studies and CRT scholars have traditionally focused on the intersection of racial and gender identities, and how racism and sexism jointly shape individual experiences. For instance, critical scholars have considered how the convergence of gendered and racial oppression shape our notions of family dynamics, roles, and responsibilities (Collins, 1998a, 1998b), as well as the societal responses to women of color who are subjected to domestic violence (Crenshaw, 1991). The work of those researchers has illustrated how women are marginalized in our society, while also highlighting the different—and at times compounding—stigma or discrimination that is experienced by women of color who often come from a less affluent socioeconomic background.

Some advocating for this approach would argue that the experiences within groups are distinctive according to the extent to which they are members of other marginalized or privileged populations, but the goal of intersectional analyses is not to develop a hierarchy of oppression that is based on the assumption that having multiple marginalized identities simply equates to more experienced discrimination (Berger and Guidroz, 2009). In other words, some might think that intersectionality suggests that a homosexual Latino male faculty member would experience double the discrimination of a heterosexual Latino or homosexual white male faculty member, but this is not the case. Rather, intersectionality suggests that the confluence of one's multiple marginalized and privileged identities is an interaction that creates a unique experience, distinctive from those with whom they may share some identities but not others (Choo and Ferree, 2010; Crenshaw, 1991). Put another way, a homosexual Latino male faculty member might not be more or less oppressed than his heterosexual Latino or gay white male counterparts; his experiences are uniquely shaped by his multiple identities and are distinct from those of his counterparts.

In the following sections, we discuss the promise of intersectionality in advancing the current state of higher education research. First, we delineate some of the salient limitations of one-dimensional analyses in higher education research. Then we discuss the role of intersectionality frameworks in addressing these limitations. Finally, we provide examples of intersectionality research in higher education to illuminate how such frameworks can advance our understandings of experiences in higher education.

One-Dimensional Analyses and the Role of Intersectionality in Higher Education Research

Although intersectionality has been a central theme and salient framework in critical feminist theory (McCall, 2005), its influence on many other academic fields, including higher education, has been limited. We do not attempt to argue that higher education researchers do not examine intersecting identities; in fact, as we discuss later in this section, researchers have advanced knowledge in the field by doing so. However, we do argue that the emphasis on intersectionality in higher education is limited and a greater emphasis on employing intersectional frameworks can contribute to important advancements in the field. For example, those who study college students are increasingly disaggregating samples by singular social identities (Pascarella and Terenzini, 2005). However, in many ways, research focusing on the unique experiences of individuals who belong to two or more social groups is still in its infancy in the field.

Overreliance on the comparison of one-dimensional analyses of individuals and groups perpetuates several limitations of higher education research and discourse. Moreover, intersectional analyses can offer a critical tool in addressing those limitations. Intersectional analyses can advance research in the field of higher education in at least four primary ways.

First, intersectionality frameworks more accurately reflect the diversity in higher education. Research that simply disaggregates college faculty by gender or college students by race does not reflect the actual diversity that exists in higher education. Racial backgrounds and sexual orientations influence the experiences of female faculty. Socioeconomic origins and citizenship status can have profound influences on the experiences of students of color. Racial categories include mixed-race individuals who identify with two, three, or four racial and ethnic backgrounds. If higher education researchers are to maximize understanding of their students, they must explore the experiences of these groups situated at the intersections of various social identities and groupings.

Second, intersectional analyses facilitate the excavation of voices and realities at the margins. Overreliance on one-dimensional categories, even though giving space to the voices of racial minorities and women in higher education, fails to establish adequate space for individuals who are situated at the margins of multiple groups. A few scholars have begun to explore the identities and experiences of those who occupy these spaces (e.g., Cooper, Ortiz, Benham, and Sherr, 2002; Cho, 2003; Harper, 2005, 2007; Museus and Kiang, 2009; Teranishi, 2010). Cho (2003), for example, demonstrates how racialized and gendered stereotypes converge to shape the unique experiences of Asian American female faculty who experience sexual harassment in the academy. Specifically, she highlights how stereotypes of Asian American women contribute to inappropriate sexual advances made by male faculty toward Asian American female faculty. Similarly, in a forthcoming counterstory, Museus (2011) highlights how a low-income female Vietnamese American student's racial, ethnic, gender, and class identities all interact to shape her unique experiences and the unique challenges that she faces while navigating the environments of a predominantly white institution. Griffin and Reddick (forthcoming) also illuminate how the racialized and gendered experiences of black male and female faculty differently influence the expectations and demands, the frequency, and the sometimes guarded nature of their interactions with students. Thus intersectional analyses can constitute a critical tool for understanding how identifying with multiple marginalized or underserved populations uniquely shape experiences and realities among individuals and groups in higher education.

Third, intersectionality promotes a greater understanding of how converging identities contribute to inequality. The failure of higher education researchers to make the intersections of social identities and groups more central in research and discourse limits the existing level of understanding of and progress in addressing equity issues in higher education. Indeed, it was not until after the beginning of the twenty-first century that many researchers in higher education began to pay attention to the intersections of race and gender. Emerging from this greater recognition was a better understanding that black male college students have the lowest graduation rate compared to all other racial and gender groups (Harper, 2006). As a result, there have been many efforts to address this inequity in higher education research and discourse (Cuyjet, 2006; Harper, 2005, 2006, 2007), and those efforts have led to insights that inform the work of institutional leaders in higher education as they construct strategies to promote success among this population.

Although there is a growing body of research on black male college students, there is a dearth of research illuminating the experiences of other groups at important identity intersections, such as women of color and LGBT students of color. We believe, however, that such attention has much to offer to the discourse that revolves around groups at the intersections of race, gender, class, and other social identities who suffer inequities in areas such as developmental outcomes, psychosocial well-being, and occupational attainment. Thus intersectional analyses can enable higher education researchers to make more prudent decisions about where to invest their energy.

Finally, intersectionality avoids simultaneous advancement and perpetuation of inequality. When researchers rely on one-dimensional categories, even their efforts to address inequities in higher education can function to perpetuate assumptions that actually contribute to other inequalities (Museus, 2009). Several scholars, for example, have highlighted the fact that discourse around addressing racial disparities in college access and success have historically functioned, whether intentionally or inadvertently, to racially exclude Asian Americans because of their high college entrance, persistence, and graduation rates relative to other racial groups (Museus, 2009; Museus and Kiang, 2009; Museus, 2011; National Commission on Asian American and Pacific Islander Research in Education [CARE], 2008, 2010; Teranishi, 2010). Those scholars have noted that most discussions of such disparities ignore that several ethnic subgroups within the Asian American population (e.g., Southeast Asian American and Pacific Islander subpopulations) suffer from drastic racial and ethnic disparities in educational attainment. Intersectional analyses can move beyond more simplistic one-dimensional analyses to ensure that particular groups are not being excluded from discussions of equity in higher education.

Conclusion

Although higher education researchers have conducted research that examines populations at the intersections of various social identities and groupings, such intersectional analyses are not yet commonplace in research and discourse in the field. Consequently, much of the promise of intersectionality research has yet to be realized in higher education. The remaining chapters in this volume constitute one small step toward realizing the potential of mixed-methods research in better understanding how multiple identities shape the experiences and outcomes of populations in higher education.

References

Berger, M. T., and Guidroz, K. (eds.). *The Intersectional Approach: Transforming the Academic Through Race, Class, and Gender*. Chapel Hill: University of North Carolina Press, 2009.

Cho, S. K. "Converging Stereotypes in Racialized Sexual Harassment: Where the Model Minority Meets Suzie Wong." In A. K. Wing (ed.), *Critical Race Feminism: A Reader* (pp. 349–356). New York: New York University Press, 2003.

Choo, H. Y., and Ferree, M. M. "Practicing Intersectionality in Sociological Research: A Critical Analysis of Inclusions, Interactions, and Institutions in the Study of Inequalities." *Sociological Theory*, 2010, 28(2), 129–149.

Collins, P. H. "Intersections of Race, Class, Gender, and Nation: Some Implications for Black Family Studies." *Journal of Comparative Family Studies*, 1998a, 29(1), 27–36.

Collins, P. H. "It's All in the Family: Intersections of Gender, Race, and Nation." *Hypatia*, 1998b, *13*(3), 62–82.

Cooper, J. E., Ortiz, A. M., Benham, M.K.P., and Sherr, M. W. "Finding a Home in the Academy: Confronting Racism and Ageism." In J. E. Cooper and D. D. Stevens (eds.), *Tenure in the Sacred Cove* (pp. 71–88). Albany: SUNY Press, 2002.

Crenshaw, K. "Demarginalizing the Intersection of Race and Sex: A Black Feminist Critique of Antidiscrimination Doctrine, Feminist Theory, and Antiracist Politics." *University of Chicago Legal Forum*, 1989, 139–167.

Crenshaw, K. "Mapping the Margins: Intersectionality, Identity Politics, and Violence Against Women of Color." *Stanford Law Review*, 1991, *43*(6), 1241–1299.

Cuyjet, M. J. (ed.). *African American Men in College*. San Francisco: Jossey-Bass, 2006.

Griffin, K. A., and Reddick, R. J. "Surveillance and Sacrifice: Gender Differences in the Mentoring Patterns of Black Professors at Predominantly White Research Universities." *American Educational Research Journal*, forthcoming.

Harper, S. R. "Leading the Way: Inside the Experiences of High-Achieving African American Male Students." *About Campus*, 2005, *10*(1), 8–15.

Harper, S. R. *Black Male Students at Public Flagship Universities in the U.S.: Status, Trends, and Implications for Policy and Practice*. Washington, D.C.: Joint Center Health Policy Institute, 2006.

Harper, S. R. "Using Qualitative Methods to Assess Student Trajectories and College Impact." In S. R. Harper and S. D. Museus (eds.), *Using Qualitative Methods in Institutional Assessment*. New Directions for Institutional Research, no. 136. San Francisco: Jossey-Bass, 2007.

Jones, S. R. "Constructing Identities at the Intersections: An Autoethnographic Exploration of Multiple Dimensions of Identity." *Journal of College Student Development*, 2009, *50*(3), 287–304.

McCall, L. "The Complexity of Intersectionality." *Journal of Women in Culture and Society*, 2005, *30*(3), 1771–1800.

Museus, S. D. "A Critical Analysis of the Exclusion of Asian American from Higher Education Research and Discourse." In L. Zhan (ed.), *Asian American Voices: Engaging, Empowering, Enabling* (pp. 59–76). New York: NLN Press, 2009.

Museus, S. D., and Kiang, P. N. "The Model Minority Myth and How It Contributes to the Invisible Minority Reality in Higher Education Research." In S. D. Museus (ed.), *Conducting Research on Asian Americans in Higher Education*. New Directions for Institutional Research, no. 142. San Francisco: Jossey-Bass, 2009.

Museus, S. D. "Voices at the Margins: A Critical Race Counternarrative of Asian American Students Navigating Exclusionary Campus Environments." Unpublished manuscript, University of Hawaii at Manoa, 2011.

National Commission on Asian American and Pacific Islander Research in Education [CARE]. *Facts, Not Fiction: Setting the Records Straight*. New York: CARE, 2008.

National Commission on Asian American and Pacific Islander Research in Education [CARE]. *Federal Higher Education Policy Priorities and the Asian American and Pacific Islander Community*. New York: CARE, 2010.

Pascarella, E. T., and Terenzini, P. T. *How College Affects Students*. Vol. 2: *A Third Decade of Research*. San Francisco: Jossey-Bass, 2005.

Ramachandran, G. "Intersectionality as 'Catch 22': Why Identity Performance Demands Are Neither Harmless Nor Reasonable." *Albany Law Review*, 2005, 69, 299–342.

Shields, S. A. "Gender: An Intersectionality Perspective." *Sex Roles*, 2008, 59, 301–311.

Teranishi, R. T. "Race, Ethnicity, and Higher Education Policy: The Use of Critical Quantitative Research." In F. Stage (ed.), *Using Quantitative Research to Answer*

Critical Questions. New Directions for Institutional Research, no. 133. San Francisco: Jossey-Bass, 2010.

Teranishi, R. T. *Asians in the Ivory Tower: Dilemmas of Racial Inequality in American Higher Education*. New York: Teachers College Press, 2010.

SAMUEL D. MUSEUS *is an assistant professor of educational administration at the University of Hawai'i Manoa.*

KIMBERLY A. GRIFFIN *is an assistant professor of education policy studies at the Pennsylvania State University and a research associate in the Center for the Study of Higher Education.*

NEW DIRECTIONS FOR INSTITUTIONAL RESEARCH • DOI: 10.1002/ir

2

In this chapter, the authors discuss the utility of mixed-methods research in conducting intersectional analyses in higher education. They also discuss challenges to conducting mixed-methods intersectionality research and offer suggestions for overcoming them.

Application of Mixed-Methods Approaches to Higher Education and Intersectional Analyses

Kimberly A. Griffin, Samuel D. Museus

As scholars argue that intersectionality—the examination of individuals and their positionality at the intersection of multiple social identities or groupings—in higher education is a research paradigm rather than just a topic of study (e.g., Dhamoon, 2011; Hancock, 2007), there has been a great deal of discussion over the modes of analysis best suited to address how multiple identities shape the lived experience. Hancock calls attention to the need for appropriate methodology for intersectional inquiry, stating that "to move beyond testing time-worn theories, to examine the as-yet unanswered questions intersectionality generates, intersectional empiricists cannot rely on the same old data, or more precisely, data collected in the same old unitary way" (p. 66). Hancock and others suggest that mixed methods, which integrate qualitative and quantitative modes of analysis, may be best suited for this for intersectional inquiry. For example, Trahan (2011) notes that the basic principles of intersectionality align well with a mixed-methods analytical strategy. Intersectionality suggests that there are multiple, overlapping systems of oppression that shape our lives and experiences in complex ways. Consequently, this complexity requires truly understanding multiple forms of data and analysis.

It has been approximately a decade since Borland (2001) and his colleagues highlighted the utility of mixed-method approaches in scholarly and institutional research. Yet mixed-methods research is still not widely adopted or used in the field of higher education. This chapter is based on

New Directions for Institutional Research, no. 151, Fall 2011 © Wiley Periodicals, Inc.
Published online in Wiley Online Library (wileyonlinelibrary.com) • DOI: 10.1002/ir.396

15

the premise that higher education researchers can benefit from a better understanding of how mixed-methods approaches can be used to study not only intersectionality but various individuals, groups, processes, relationships, and phenomena in postsecondary education more generally.

Mixed-methods research can be defined in many ways (Creswell and Plano Clark, 2007; Johnson and Onwuegbuzie, 2004; Johnson, Onwuegbuzie, and Turner, 2007; Tashakkori and Teddlie, 1998). For the purposes of this chapter, we rely on the definition of *mixed-methods research* as "the type of research in which a researcher or team of researchers combines elements of quantitative and qualitative research approaches (e.g., use of quantitative and qualitative viewpoints, data collection, analysis, inference techniques) for the broad purposes of breadth and depth of understanding and corroboration" (Johnson, Onwuegbuzie, and Turner, 2007, p.123). This definition of mixed-methods research excludes multimethod designs, in which researchers mix multiple quantitative (e.g., surveys and structured observations) or qualitative (e.g., data from interviews and documents) forms of data (Creswell and Plano Clark, 2007).

In the remainder of this chapter, we discuss the utility of combining quantitative and qualitative methods in conducting intersectional analyses (see Chapter One for complete discussion of intersectionality research). First, we discuss some of the paradigmatic underpinnings of qualitative and quantitative research, and how these methods can be used in intersectional analyses. We then consider how paradigmatic pragmatism informs mixed-methods research, which can be an alternative research strategy that mitigates some of the limitations of mono-method quantitative and qualitative studies of intersectionality in higher education. Next, we present important choices that researchers must make in designing mixed-method research, followed by descriptions of four mixed-methods designs that can be used in conducting intersectional analyses in postsecondary education. Finally, we discuss challenges that researchers who conduct mixed-methods intersectionality research might face and provide some recommendations to address those challenges.

Mono-Methods and Intersectionality Research

Mixed-methods emerged from and function to integrate quantitative and qualitative methods. Quantitative and qualitative methods have much in common—researchers use both types of methods to describe data, analyze and construct explanations from data, and make inferences based on those data (Sechrest and Sidani, 1995)—but the differences between these two paradigms have, more often than not, been the focus of scholarly discourse. Table 2.1 is based on previous literature (e.g., Creswell and Plano Clark, 2007; Johnson and Onwuegbuzie, 2004; Johnson, Onwuegbuzie, and Turner, 2007) and outlines some of these distinctions. As the table shows, quantitative and qualitative paradigms differ in their philosophical

NEW DIRECTIONS FOR INSTITUTIONAL RESEARCH • DOI: 10.1002/ir

Table 2.1. Juxtaposition of Quantitative and Qualitative Paradigms

Quantitative	Component of Research Process	Qualitative
• Positivist: singular reality independent of researcher	**Ontology and epistemology**	• Constructivist: multiple realities dependent upon researcher
• Test hypotheses • Test and validating theory • Prediction • Identify and confirm existence of relationships • Generalize to population • Isolate focal variables or relationships	**Purposes and nature of inquiry**	• Understand and explain experiences, processes, events, and other phenomena • Provide rich description • Generate theory • Consider complexity and context of phenomena
• Large and random	**Participant samples**	• Small and purposeful
• Numerical (e.g., surveys, structured observations)	**Data collection techniques**	• Textual or pictorial (e.g., participant observations, individual and focus group interviews, documents)
• Statistical analyses	**Data analysis techniques**	• Textural or pictorial analyses
• Internal validity (i.e., accurate measurement), external validity (i.e., generalizablity), and reliability (i.e., consistent measurement)	**Assessment of quality**	• Credibility (i.e., accurate representation of participant reality) and transferability (i.e., ability to infer results can be transferred to other contexts)
• Removed from process to maximize objectivity	**Role of researcher**	• Engaged in subjective process
• Lacks detail and context • May miss reality because of the focus on testing and validity preexisting	**Limitations of approach**	• Not generalizable • Time-consuming • More easily influenced by researcher bias

foundations, purposes, data collection and analysis techniques, role of researchers, and limitations.

Pure quantitative and qualitative researchers have traditionally subscribed to different paradigms, which include various beliefs about what constitutes reality (i.e., ontology) and how knowledge is constructed (i.e., epistemology; Johnson and Onwuegbuzie, 2004; Jones, Torres, and Arminio, 2006; Tashakkori and Teddlie, 1998). The perspectives of quantitative researchers are often rooted in positivism, which, in its purest form, suggests that there is a single reality to be explored and identified through objective research. Pure positivists argue that the knower and the known are independent; they charge that research can and should be value-free. Positivists also believe researchers can use quantitative methods to establish cause-and-effect relationships that can be generalized across time and context (Johnson and Onwuegbuzie, 2004; Tashakkori and Teddlie, 1998).

Postpositivism emerged in the 1950s and tempered many of the positivist beliefs about the value-laden nature of research and social construction of reality; constructivism was developed as a more radical response to positivism (Tashakkori and Teddlie, 1998). Endorsed largely by qualitatively oriented scholars, the tenets of constructivism are quite distinctive from the beliefs often embraced by positivists. Constructivists believe that multiple, individually constructed realities exist and see the knower and information to be known as inseparable. Research and knowledge are seen as value-laden, highly influenced by the beliefs of researchers. The subjectivity of inquiry and knowledge eliminates the ability to generalize across time and context. Constructivists also believe causes and effects cannot be distinguished from one another, and that our understandings of the world should be generated through an inductive process, starting with observations, which are used to develop theory (Johnson and Onwuegbuzie, 2004; Tashakkori and Teddlie, 1998).

In the context of intersectionality research, both quantitative and qualitative methods can offer tools that generate rich insights depending on the research question being asked and the purpose of the inquiry. For example, quantitative research methods can be used for several purposes in intersectional analyses.

Category Comparison. Higher education scholars and institutional researchers can use quantitative techniques to identify inequities that exist at the intersections of multiple social identities or groupings. For example, postsecondary researchers can compare the persistence and degree attainment rates of all gender and racial groups to understand which populations suffer from inequities when considering those two types of social groupings (e.g. see Harper, 2006).

Category Deconstruction. Related to category comparison, researchers can disaggregate quantitative data to analyze subgroups within a particular category to generate a more complex picture of reality than is presented when the entire racial category is examined (e.g. see Museus, 2009; Museus and Kiang, 2009; Teranishi, 2010).

Generalizability Assessment. Higher education scholars and institutional researchers can quantify the findings of a qualitative inquiry into the experiences of a person or persons who are situated at the intersection of social identities or groupings to assess whether those findings are generalizable to the larger population at that intersection.

Qualitative methods also have significant utility in conducting intersectionality research. They can, for example, serve several purposes.

Voice Excavation. Higher education researchers can use qualitative approaches to excavate the unique voices of those who are situated at the intersections of multiple social identities and groupings, which can illuminate their unique experiences and realities that might otherwise remain unheard (e.g., see Crenshaw, 1991).

Disparity Explanation. Researchers can also use qualitative methods to answer questions regarding why particular groups at social identity intersections suffer from disparities in areas such as psychosocial well-being, moral and civic development, or postgraduate educational and occupational success.

Paradigmatic Pragmatism, Mixed Methods, and Intersectionality

Despite their potential utility in conducting intersectional analyses, both quantitative and qualitative approaches have significant limitations, particularly when engaging in intersectional analyses. Quantitative methods have perhaps received the most attention for their limitations, being critiqued as inadequate to address the integrative, complex nature of identity (Bowleg, 2008; Dhamoon, 2011; Hancock, 2007; Trahan, 2011). The disaggregation required by quantitative analysis tends to frame identity in an additive rather than integrative way and tends to ignore differences within identity groups (Hancock, 2007; Trahan, 2011). Scholars have asserted the importance of qualitative strategies to intersectional analyses (e.g. Bowleg, 2008; Hancock, 2007; Traham 2011); however, qualitative methods are not without their limitations. In addition to being time- and cost-intensive, data can be challenging to interpret; it can also be hard to understand how the specific dimensions are coming together or are most salient in a particular experience (Bowleg, 2008).

Mixed methods can serve as a useful methodological alternative and have the potential to maximize the benefits and balance the limitations of both qualitative and quantitative strategies (Hancock, 2007; Johnson and Onwuegbuzie, 2004; Trahan, 2011). Mixed methodology is based on a third epistemological orientation: paradigmatic pragmatism. Tashakkori and Teddlie (1998) describe paradigmatic "purists" as espousing the fundamental belief that qualitative and quantitative methods are incompatible and impossible to integrate because they are based on oppositional para-digms (i.e., positivism and constructivism). Paradigmatic pragmatism, however, advocates for an epistemological middle ground. Paradigmatic pragmatists do not posit that reality is absolute or entirely based on the perceptions of individuals. Rather, they assert that knowledge is simulta-neously constructed and based on a general reality that we all inhabit (Johnson and Onwuegbuzie, 2004). Pragmatists acknowledge that values shape how researchers determine what to study and the nature of their analyses, but they do not perceive this subjectivity as problematic because research can be conducted to meet specific value-based needs (Johnson and Onwuegbuzie, 2004; Morgan, 2007; Tashakkori and Teddlie, 1998). Pragmatists also believe in the existence of causal relationships but acknowledge that these are extremely difficult to clarify and identify because they are influenced by context, which is constantly changing (Cherryholmes, 1994).

Paradigmatic pragmatists believe in the utility of collecting both numerical and textual data to address complex problems. They highlight the similarities, rather than the distinctions, between constructivists and positivists (Johnson and Onwuegbuzie, 2004). Absence of commitment to one philosophical worldview allows pragmatists to integrate the assump-tions and strategies of both qualitative and quantitative researchers (Creswell, 2003) to construct a design that is best suited to address the research questions and fulfill the purpose of the research at hand. This aligns well with the principles undergirding intersectionality. According to Hancock (2007), intersectionality resides in a philosophical space similar to pragmatism, standing "ontologically between reductionist research that blindly seeks only the generalizable and particularized research so special-ized it cannot contribute to theory" (p. 74).

When used in intersectional analyses, mixed-methods strategies can allow researchers to gain a broader and deeper understanding of the multi-dimensional nature of identity and its role in students', professors', and administrators' lives. Mixed methods are a relatively new form of research design, but they are increasingly used to gain more holistic understand-ings of complex phenomena from multiple perspectives (Creswell and Plano Clark, 2007), which may constitute a powerful methodological strategy for intersectional analyses. Researchers, for instance, can use quantitative methods to identify groups that suffer from disparities and qualitative methods to illuminate the voices of individuals within that group.

Mixed-methods design also allows researchers to balance the weak-nesses of one methodology with the strengths of another (Creswell and Plano Clark, 2007; Johnson and Onwuegbuzie, 2004; Tashakkori and Teddlie, 1998). Quantitative data offers precision, is efficient for studying large groups, and can be an effective way to test hypotheses. However, quantitative work does not necessarily address why or how phenomena occur. Further, these methods often ignore how culture or common under-standings within a community, which are difficult to quantify, can shape the relationships between variables and outcomes (Johnson and Onwueg-buzie, 2004). Qualitative methods can alleviate many of these issues, per-mitting in-depth understandings that are rich with detail. Qualitative research is known for its consideration of contextual and situational fac-tors, ability to generate theory, and utility in facilitating our understanding of how others make meaning of various phenomena. Yet the findings of qualitative research are not generalizable across contexts, are more subject to the bias of the researcher, and are time-intensive, making them ineffi-cient when aiming to understand large populations (Johnson and Onwuegbuzie, 2004)—limitations for which quantitative methods can compensate. Thus, in many ways integrating both strategies in one study maximizes opportunities to conduct studies with both depth and generalizability.

Considerations in Mixed-Methods Research Design

There are several issues to consider when designing mixed-methods research. Consistent with a pragmatist epistemology, design decisions must be made according to what would create the most informative data-set to answer the research questions that guide the inquiry. In this section, we discuss four critical decisions that must be made by those engaging in mixed-methods research: (1) the emphasis placed on qualitative and quan-titative methods, (2) sequencing of qualitative and quantitative methods, (3) how the data are integrated, and (4) the purpose of mixing.

Emphasis. In designing mixed-methods studies, researchers must consider whether the qualitative or quantitative components of the study will be given greater emphasis (Jones, Torres, and Arminio, 2006; Morgan, 1998; Morse, 1991; Tashakkori and Teddlie, 1998). Researchers may choose to give dominant status to one method if it is more fundamental to answering the research question and the other is supportive in nature. Therefore, researchers can make one of three choices: (1) qualitative data collection and analysis can be dominant, (2) quantitative data collection and analysis can be dominant, or (3) the strategies can have equivalent status (Creswell and Plano Clark, 2007; Tashakkori and Teddlie, 1998).

Sequencing. Perhaps one of the most important questions that researchers must address in designing their studies is whether data should be collected and analyzed concurrently or sequentially (Johnson and Onwuegbuzie, 2004; Johnson, Onwuegbuzie, and Turner, 2007; Leech and Onwuegbuzie, 2009). In a concurrent data collection strategy, the qualita-tive and quantitative data are collected independently and roughly at the same time (Creswell and Plano Clark, 2007; Jones, Torres, and Arminio, 2006). Alternatively, researchers can choose to collect and analyze qualita-tive data in the first phase and quantitative data in the second phase, or vice versa (i.e., sequentially). The decision regarding the sequencing of collecting and analyzing quantitative and qualitative data is closely related to the last consideration we discuss in this section: the purpose of method mixing.

Method of Mixing. The third major consideration for researchers who design mixed-methods research is how they will mix their data. There are at least three types of mixing (Creswell and Plano Clark, 2007). Researchers can (1) merge the quantitative and qualitative datasets together, (2) connect the two datasets with one building on the other, or (3) embed one dataset within another, in which case the former is designed to support the latter.

Purpose of Mixing. Finally, researchers must consider the purpose of incorporating both quantitative and qualitative methods into their analysis (Creswell and Plano Clark, 2007; Johnson and Onwuegbuzie, 2004; Johnson, Onwuegbuzie, and Turner, 2007; Leech and Onwuegbuzie, 2009; Tashakkori and Teddlie, 1998). Researchers can determine that both quantitative and qualitative methods are necessary to (1) use each method to validate the data gathered by the other, (2) use one method to inform another (e.g., use qualitative data to construct a questionnaire), (3) use one method to expand on the findings of another, (4) seek paradoxes or new perspectives, or (5) maximize the probability of generating useful findings.

Applying Mixed-Methods Designs to Intersectionality Research in Higher Education

The decisions researchers make regarding these four considerations will be reflected in and shaped by the form of mixed-methods design implemented. Given the many types of mixed-methods designs, however, it should be kept in mind that any single typology will most likely not encompass all mixed-methods designs. Nevertheless, we present four designs outlined by Cresswell and Plano Clark (2007) to give readers a framework for understanding the diversity of mixed-methods approaches that can be applied to intersectionality research. In doing so, we offer examples of how those designs might be applied to a study of intersectionality within the context of higher education.

Triangulation Designs. The goal of the triangulation design is to obtain complimentary qualitative and quantitative data on a topic to use the strengths of both methods (Morse, 1991). In this design, researchers collect both quantitative and qualitative data in a single phase to either compare and contrast findings or expand on quantitative results with qualitative findings (Creswell and Plano Clark, 2007). For example, a researcher could separately collect qualitative and quantitative data on LGBT racial minority students' perceptions of the campus climate. The qualitative and quantitative data would then be integrated into the analysis, comparing and contrasting the findings generated by each approach.

NEW DIRECTIONS FOR INSTITUTIONAL RESEARCH • DOI: 10.1002/ir

Data triangulation designs are cases in which researchers merge quantitative and qualitative findings during interpretation, validate quantitative survey results with open-ended survey questions, or use methods that vary according to the level of a system being studied (Creswell and Plano Clark, 2007). Another form of triangulation design is when researchers collect quantitative and qualitative data and then transform one type of data into the other form. For example, researchers could conduct interviews with LGBT racial minority students about their experiences with prejudice and discrimination on campus, and then quantify the extent of experienced prejudice and discrimination so that it can be correlated with those participants' responses on a quantitative survey. Thus, by transforming the qualitative data into numbers, researchers can corroborate the findings that emerge from each method or correlate findings from the quantitative component with the qualitative aspect of the investigation.

Embedded Designs. In an embedded design, researchers use secondary methods to support another dominant method (Creswell and Plano Clark, 2007). Embedded designs include cases in which researchers use qualitative data to support a quantitative experiment or use qualitative data to explain correlations that are examined in a correlational analysis. For example, researchers might use qualitative methods to develop a diversity workshop focused on LGBT racial minority issues that can be used in a quantitative experiment to test the effect of the workshop on students' prejudicial attitudes. In this case, the qualitative methods are used to support and prepare for the primary component of the research design: the experiment.

Explanatory Designs. In an explanatory design, qualitative data is used to expand on the findings generated by a quantitative analysis. This design is particularly useful when researchers would like to explain findings generated in a quantitative analysis or recruit participants with certain characteristics before engaging them in focus groups or interviews (Creswell and Plano Clark, 2007). For example, researchers interested in using an explanatory design could first conduct a regression analysis of survey data examining the relationships between LGBT racial minority students' experiences with prejudice and discrimination and satisfaction in college, and then gain a deeper understanding of the nature of prejudice and discrimination experienced by this group by conducting student focus groups.

Exploratory Designs. In mixed-methods studies with an exploratory design, the qualitative data collection and analysis precedes the quantitative analysis. This design is best for studies where the goal is to explore new phenomena, as well as to generate theories and the instruments to test them (Creswell and Plano Clark, 2007). It can also be used to confirm whether a qualitative finding within one sample is more generalizable to a wider population. One example of an exploratory design is if researchers interested in LGBT racial minority students' experiences with prejudice and discrimination conduct focus groups with students on how they experience prejudice and discrimination on campus, and then develop a quantitative survey that is based on the findings generated from the qualitative focus group data.

Dealing with the Challenges of Mixed-Methods Intersectional Analyses

Although mixed-methods designs have much utility for both higher education scholars and institutional researchers (Borland, 2001), there are several challenges. In this section, we discuss some of the challenges associated with implementing mixed-methods designs and offer recommendations to address those issues for higher education researchers who would like to integrate qualitative and quantitative methods as they engage in intersectional analyses.

Conceptual Complexity. Intersectionality research is inherently complex (McCall, 2005). For each social identity (e.g., gender, race, ethnicity, etc.) that is incorporated into a specific analysis, there is an added level of complexity. Moreover, mixed-methods designs constitute an added layer of intricacy, because researchers have to incorporate both quantitative and qualitative methods. To address this complexity, researchers should consider focusing on the intersection of two or three social identities. If the focus expands to the intersection of four or more social identities, the analysis can become increasingly complex, rendering it difficult to make sense of data. Although it is likely researchers will have to deal with a significant amount of complexity regardless, limiting the number of identities considered within the study can provide parameters that somewhat diminish complexity with which researchers must deal when conducting mixed-methods intersectionality research.

Required Expertise. Conducting mixed-methods research requires sufficient expertise in quantitative, qualitative, and mixed-methods research. Researchers not only must be able to collect and analyze both quantitative and qualitative data, but they must also possess the ability to design a mixed-methods inquiry and integrate quantitative and qualitative methods. If researchers are primarily quantitative or qualitative, or they have limited familiarity with mixed methods, they might want to consider collaboration with colleagues who have more knowledge and expertise. Alternatively, researchers can hire consultants who are knowledgeable about quantitative, qualitative, and mixed methods for support to mitigate some of the challenges associated with learning and executing new and unfamiliar methodologies.

Resource Requirements. In many—but not all—cases, mixed-methods research requires more resources (e.g., time, money, energy) than implementing solely quantitative or qualitative research designs because mixed-methods studies require collection and analysis of both quantitative and qualitative data. This means that mixed-methods studies can present situations in which researchers are, in essence, conducting two complimentary inquiries, both of which require substantial resources. There are several ways to address this resource challenge. Researchers can use existing datasets (e.g., see Chapters Four and Six). Or if existing datasets are not available, researchers can integrate the two components of their mixed-methods inquiry to the extent possible by, for example, soliciting participants for the second component of the study during the first phase of the inquiry in sequential designs. This can reduce the amount of energy required for recruitment.

Conclusion

Both intersectionality and mixed-methods research designs are underused in higher education research. For progress to be made in this area, higher education researchers must consider and discuss the various ways in which mixed-methods approaches can be applied to examining groups, processes, and phenomena in colleges and universities. In this chapter, we discuss the utility of mixed-methods designs generally, but also specifically within the context of conducting intersectional analyses, with the hope that this will build the foundation for inquiries of this nature in scholarly and institutional research. Mixed-methods hold great potential to illuminate the complexity associated with the multiple identities of students, faculty, and staff coming together in unique ways to shape their development, experiences, and outcomes in higher education. Though not without methodological challenges, mixed-methods techniques address the limitations of reliance on qualitative or quantitative methods alone, as demonstrated in the remaining chapters in this volume.

References

Borland, K. W., Jr. "Qualitative and Quantitative Research: A Complimentary Balance." In K. W. Borland, Jr. (ed.), *Balancing Qualitative and Quantitative Information for Effective Decision Support*. New Directions for Institutional Research, no. 112. San Francisco: Jossey-Bass, 2001.

Bowleg, L. "When Black + Lesbian + Woman ≠ Black Lesbian Woman: The Methodological Challenges of Qualitative and Quantitative Intersectionality Research." *Sex Roles*, 2008, 59, 312–325.

Cherryholmes, C. H. "More Notes on Pragmatism." *Educational Researcher*, 1994, 23(1), 16–18.

Crenshaw, K. "Mapping the Margins: Intersectionality, Identity Politics, and Violence Against Women of Color." *Stanford Law Review*, 1991, 43(6), 1241–1299.

Creswell, J. W. *Research Design: Qualitative, Quantitative, and Mixed-Methods Approaches* (2nd ed.). Thousand Oaks, Calif.: Sage, 2003.

Creswell, J. W., and Plano Clark, V. L. *Designing and Conducting Mixed-Methods Research*. Thousand Oaks, Calif.: Sage, 2007.

Dhamoon, R. K. "Considerations of Mainstreaming Intersection." *Political Research Quarterly*, 2011, 64(1), 230–243.

Hancock, A. "Where Multiplication Doesn't Equal Quick Addition: Examining Inter-sectionality as a Research Paradigm." *Perspectives on Politics*, 2007, *5*(1), 63–79.

Harper, S. R. *Black Male Students at Public Flagship Universities in the U.S.: Status, Trends, and Implications for Policy and Practice.* Washington, D.C.: Joint Center Health Policy Institute, 2006.

Johnson, R. B., and Onwuegbuzie, A. J. (2004). Mixed-Methods Research: A Research Paradigm Whose Time Has Come." *Educational Researcher, 33*(7), 14–26.

Johnson, R. B., Onwuegbuzie, A. J., and Turner, L. A. "Toward a Definition of Mixed-Methods Research." *Journal of Mixed-Methods Research*, 2007, *1*(2), 112–133.

Jones, S. R., Torres, V., and Arminio, J. *Negotiating the Complexities of Qualitative Research in Higher Education: Fundamental Elements and Issues.* New York: Routledge, 2006.

Leech, N. L., and Onwuegbuzie, A. J. "A Typology of Mixed-Methods Research Designs." *Quality and Quantity,* 2009, *43,* 265–275.

McCall, L. "The Complexity of Intersectionality." *Signs: Journal of Women in Culture and Society*, 2005, *30*(31), 1771–1800.

Morgan, D. L. "Practical Strategies for Combining Qualitative and Quantitative Methods: Applications to Health Research." *Qualitative Health Research,* 1998, *3,* 362–376.

Morgan, D. L. "Paradigms Lost and Pragmatism Regained: Methodological Implications of Combining Qualitative and Quantitative Methods." *Journal of Mixed-Methods Research,* 2007, *1*(1), 48–76.

Morse, J. M. "Approaches to Qualitative-Quantitative Methodological Triangulation." *Nursing Research,* 1991, *40,* 120–123.

Museus, S. D. "A Critical Analysis of the Exclusion of Asian American from Higher Education Research and Discourse." In L. Zhan (ed.), *Asian American Voices: Engaging, Empowering, Enabling* (pp. 59–76). New York: NLN Press, 2009.

Museus, S. D., and Kiang, P. N. "The Model Minority Myth and How It Contributes to the Invisible Minority Reality in Higher Education Research." In S. D. Museus (ed.), *Conducting Research on Asian Americans in Higher Education.* New Directions for Institutional Research, no. 142. San Francisco: Jossey-Bass, 2009.

Sechrest, L., and Sidani, S. "Quantitative and Qualitative Methods: Is There an Alternative?" *Evaluation and Program Planning,* 1995, *18,* 77–87.

Tashakkori, A., and Teddlie, C. *Mixed-Methodology: Combining Qualitative and Quantitative Approaches* (Vol. 46). Thousand Oaks, Calif.: Sage, 1998.

Teranishi, R. T. *Asians in the Ivory Tower: Dilemmas of Racial Inequality in American Higher Education.* New York: Teachers College Press, 2010.

Trahan, A. "Qualitative Research and Intersectionality." *Critical Criminology,* 2011, *19,* 1–14.

KIMBERLY A. GRIFFIN *is an assistant professor of education policy studies at the Pennsylvania State University and a research associate in the Center for the Study of Higher Education.*

SAMUEL D. MUSEUS *is an assistant professor of educational administration at the University of Hawai'i Manoa.*

NEW DIRECTIONS FOR INSTITUTIONAL RESEARCH • DOI: 10.1002/ir

3

This chapter describes intersectionality as it relates to faculty careers, and a mixed-methods approach to researching faculty members' identities in departmental contexts.

Intersectionality in Context: A Mixed-Methods Approach to Researching the Faculty Experience

Meghan J. Pifer

Even though many researchers have broadly studied "the faculty experience," this chapter focuses on faculty members' interactions and relationships, specifically within the context of the academic department. Collegial relationships between faculty members in institutional and departmental contexts can be understood as social networks, or groups of people linked by social relationships. A network perspective on organizations focuses on relationships and structured patterns of interaction between individual actors in a given social or organizational context (Brass, Galaskiewicz, Greve, and Tsai, 2004). In other words, the study of faculty members and their social networks explores who they interact with and for what reasons. Departmental networks include formal interactions, such as those structured around individual and departmental tasks related to teaching, research, and service activities. They can also include informal interactions, such as friendships and mentoring relationships, casual conversations in faculty lounges and meetings, departmental and institutional social events, and even observed or shared accounts of incidents on campus.

Social networks are important to faculty work and life. The availability of networking opportunities is a significant contributor to subjective assessments of career success among faculty members (Peluchette, 1993). As in most organizational settings, faculty members rely on their networks to access resources such as friendship, mentoring, advice, information, ties

New Directions for Institutional Research, no. 151, Fall 2011 © Wiley Periodicals, Inc.
Published online in Wiley Online Library (wileyonlinelibrary.com) • DOI: 10.1002/ir.397

27

to powerful people, and opportunities for professional advancement (Di Leo, 2003; Poole and Bornholt, 1998). As much as positive relationships can provide access to such resources, negative relationships or exclusion from relationships can cause stress, barriers to information, feelings of isolation, and missed professional opportunities such as participation in co-teaching, collaborative research, or co-publishing.

In addition to their outcomes at the individual level, faculty experiences within their networks on campus can have a significant impact on institution-level outcomes. The consequences of the behaviors and experiences of an institution's faculty members can affect the institution in such diverse and important areas as quality of teaching and research, institutional reputation, student recruitment, grants and funding, and alumni relations. Individual and institutional characteristics interact and give faculty members the tools to create meaning in their work and to understand their professional and personal experiences on campus. That meaning and understanding, in turn, affects faculty behavior and attitudes, such as their intent to stay, collaboration with colleagues, and engagement with students. Faculty behaviors and attitudes also affect institutions in terms of tenure success rate, student experiences with faculty, campus climate, and institutional reputation (for example, being an employer that offers benefits to same-sex partners or on-campus child care facilities). Further, faculty experiences result in institution-specific outcomes that will influence current and future ability to recruit, retain, and support a strong faculty. A satisfied, successful, and diverse faculty is also important for institutional relationships with prospective students, donors, funding agencies, potential employees, and other stakeholders involved in the success of the institution.

This chapter describes a mixed-methods approach to integrating the methodological tools of social network analysis and qualitative research to explore intersectionality as it pertains to faculty experiences in institutional contexts. These research strategies, employed at the individual and aggregate levels, can be useful tools as institutions aim to promote better individual and institutional outcomes of faculty members' experiences within the local context of the academic department. Studies exploring faculty interactions and relationships at the individual level would enhance understanding of how professors' identities shape their experiences, and the consequences of identity for the formation of social networks and relationships. For example, attention to faculty identity and networks can add insight into what it is like to be pregnant on the tenure track, or the only person of color working in a lab. There is, in fact, a helpful and growing body of research in this area (e.g., Lester, 2008; Griffin, Pifer, Humphrey, and Hazelwood, 2011). Institutional researchers may also want to explore individual experiences and outcomes in the aggregate to improve general understandings of the faculty experience within colleges and universities. For example, studies about the relationship between identity and networks can be extremely useful to institutional leaders who seek information about how to replicate the cases of faculty who are extremely satisfied and productive. Research about the average experience of faculty members across campus should also explore whether there is, in fact, an average experience that promotes an inclusive understanding of the structure and outcomes of interactions with peers and colleagues.

Research in this area can also be used to improve the experiences of those who do not feel at home on their campuses. In light of the increasing number of faculty members from underrepresented or previously absent groups populating today's colleges and universities, institutional researchers could benefit from greater understanding of how faculty members' experiences are shaped by their multiple identities within institutional contexts and cultures. Here, we can consider how attention to intersectionality may help us understand the potential for institutionalized inequity through employment trends, evaluation practices, mentoring programs, tenure and promotion policies, and other components of institutional involvement in the faculty career. Explorations of intersectionality in academic careers may illuminate the professional and personal challenges faced by faculty members whose multiple identities are not reflected in the collective identity of the department or institution, or who feel like outsiders within their scholarly homes because of the groups with which they most closely identify.

Intersectionality and Faculty Careers

Although institutional researchers have not fully capitalized on the usefulness of the intersectionality framework to understand the faculty experience within institutional contexts, scholars have laid the foundation for its applicability. Intersectionality emerged through the work of scholars who challenged the feminist perspective as representing the white, majority female experience and ignoring other intersecting identities that can define women's experiences (Crenshaw, 1991; Shields, 2008). When applied to the study of faculty careers, this may be understood as a need to explore not just "the faculty experience," which may assume a majority perspective, but the faculty experience across intersecting identities, which may give voice to experiences within and across categories of difference. Hancock (2007a) identified the key objective of intersectional work as "incorporating previously ignored and excluded populations into preexisting frameworks to broaden our knowledge base" (p. 248). This objective of inclusion reminds us first of the populations that historically have been excluded from the professoriate, and second that researchers should be cognizant of opportunities to strengthen knowledge about the faculty as a whole by researching the experiences of its members across various identities and characteristics.

NEW DIRECTIONS FOR INSTITUTIONAL RESEARCH • DOI: 10.1002/ir

Institutional researchers may not be fully able to understand the faculty experience and how it relates to institutional outcomes if they fail to consider the intersectional identities that shape faculty experiences and perceptions within institutional contexts. Crenshaw (1991) wrote that practitioners who seek to understand the experiences of specific populations are likely to encounter "failure, frustration, and burnout" if they do not include intersecting identities in their approach (p. 1251). She encouraged the use of intersectionality "to summon the courage to challenge groups that are after all, in one sense, 'home' to us, in the name of the parts of us that are not made at home" (p. 1299). Her attention to identity politics, the potential for internal exclusion, and the processes by which a group's identity is constructed from those of its members has strong implications for understanding intersectionality in the faculty experience. Perry (2009) called attention to occupational stereotyping, and the resulting reproduction of practices and policies "that allow for discriminatory hiring practices; unfair evaluations of workers, and the segmentation and segregation of workers along gender, race, or socioeconomic class statuses" (p. 238). Further, Fitts (2009) urged administrators to embrace the importance of recognizing scholars' complete and intersecting identities into the structure of academic units. She offered some guidance about the institutionalization of intersectionality, which includes methodological examination of "the extent to which institutions reflect difference and are self-reflexive about how that difference (or lack thereof) impacts their deliverables [including] recruitment, promotion, and tenure" (p. 256).

Researching Intersectionality and the Faculty Experience

There are two approaches that may be beneficial for defining intersectionality for the purposes of institutional research. First, the researcher may choose to define the intersection of specific identities, such as race and gender or nationality and age. This creates opportunities to explore characteristics and relationships that may be of particular significance in a given context or in response to a specific research question (McCall, 2005). Through this approach, institutional researchers can collect data about intersections that may not otherwise be emphasized in faculty members' accounts of their professional experiences.

Some scholars have expressed concern, however, that a predetermined emphasis on certain identities favors the researcher's point of view over that of the participant (Abes, Jones, and McEwen, 2007) or excludes key intersections by highlighting others (McCall, 2005). As Torres, Jones, and Renn (2009) pointed out, "it is difficult for participants to fully articulate intersectional identities" (p. 590). The researcher is left with the authority and responsibility to interpret intersectionality as it relates to faculty experiences and the institutional structures and cultures within which they interact. For example, institutional researchers interested in exploring the role of tenure status and gender in the faculty experience may be able to develop a rich understanding of some dynamics, but they may fail to identify and acknowledge other influential factors such as race, family responsibilities, leadership styles, or departmental norms because of their own beliefs and assumptions about the aspects of identity most central in faculty work.

Much attention has been given to the intersection of race and gender in society, but there is a range of characteristics that may become salient in the construction of intersecting identities (Shields, 2008), particularly in the academy. Personal characteristics such as race, ethnicity, nationality, gender, age, marital status, sexual orientation, and parenting or caregiving roles can all intersect meaningfully to affect professors' experiences at their campuses. Professional characteristics can also affect how faculty members perceive themselves and their colleagues, and make sense of their experiences within their departments and institutions. Such characteristics include rank, tenure status, administrative and leadership roles, methodological orientations, research agendas, and teaching styles and interests. Thus, without asking faculty members about which of their identities are most salient to them, researchers may be missing a large part of understanding how institutional structures and the networks of relationships that exist within them shape faculty experiences.

To address this issue, researchers can design studies that allow participants to identify and explain which components of their identities are most salient to them. This approach can be helpful because "the researcher may not always know a priori what intersections will end up playing a role in the research experience" (Warner, 2008, p. 457). The role of the analyst in this approach is "to make explicit the often implicit experiences of intersectionality, even when participants do not express the connections" (Bowleg, 2008, p. 322). The challenge of this approach is the unpredictability and lack of focus that may result from complete reliance on participants' provision of data about intersectionality as they choose to define or describe it; however, it is perhaps a more accurate reflection of participants' beliefs about the salience of their identities in their professional lives.

A Mixed-Methods Approach: Network Surveys and Individual Interviews

Understanding how faculty members determine the salience of intersecting components of their identities in institutional contexts is no easy task. Institutional researchers have advocated for the use of mixed-methods studies to explore answers to not only what occurs but also how and why it occurs (Howard, 2007). A mixed-methods approach to researching faculty experiences may illuminate the institution-specific variables that affect faculty members' abilities to see themselves as capable, accepted, and rewarded members of their departments and institutions.

Using a mixed-methods research design, integrating social network analysis and qualitative strategies, allows researchers to obtain and analyze data in multiple ways to acquire a rich and complex understanding of how faculty identities are related to the faculty career and relevant institutional outcomes. Social network analysis provides a tool for quantifying relationships in ways that can illuminate patterns and trends in faculty interactions. In addition to helping researchers identify who is most or least connected to colleagues, the network perspective can also yield data that allows a numerical comparison of networks within a given organizational structure, such as an academic department. For example, data from the social network surveys discussed in this chapter indicated the number of ties each participant had to his or her departmental colleagues, as well as the number of connections developed for the specific functions of their work. Qualitative research methods permit exploration of questions such as how and why faculty members form the networking behaviors and relationships they do. By collecting both social network data and qualitative data, researchers can develop a rich understanding of the structures, development, nature, and outcomes of professional relationships within institutional contexts.

One benefit of exploring intersectionality through the mixed-methods approach is the opportunity to explore characteristics within institutional contexts as defined by the researcher while simultaneously supporting the emergence of previously unidentified or unacknowledged dimensions of identity through participants' accounts of their experiences. Combining social network data with qualitative data may allow researchers to obtain otherwise unavailable information about intersecting identities within higher education contexts.

There are also theoretical similarities between intersectionality and social network research that make this form of analysis appealing. Both perspectives can be used to explore the replication of power structures and oppression/opportunity in social contexts. In her discussion of intersectionality, Shields (2008) wrote that those who are advantaged by certain intersections benefit from "access to rewards, status, and opportunities unavailable to other intersections" (p. 302). The role of networks in careers and broader social contexts is described in similar terms, including interactions with colleagues according to perceived similarity or difference to oneself, the salience of individual characteristics as defined by social context, access to or barriers from resources based on network position, and relative power and influence based on comparative social positioning.

Research Example

To illustrate this type of research, I describe a recent study of twenty-one tenure-track faculty members in two academic departments within one research university. The conceptual framework for the study was influenced by Ibarra's work on the development of networks among women and minorities in management (1993), and Finkelstein's research (1982) about the functions of colleagueship among faculty members. Ibarra developed a model for exploring the factors that shape network structures, which emphasized the characteristics of both individuals and the organizations in which their networks exist. When considering the experiences of faculty members within their departments, organizational factors such as institutional culture, departmental leadership, disciplinary influence, and tenure and promotion systems can influence the reasons faculty members interact with each other. Finkelstein's work is a helpful framework for conceptualizing these motivations, and it suggested five colleagueship functions: (1) help in teaching; (2) help in research; (3) institutional policies and politics; (4) disciplinary linkage (e.g., identifying sources of research support); and (5) general support, intellectual stimulation, and friendship.

For this study, I collected and analyzed data about the departments (e.g., leadership roles and processes within departments; numbers and ratios of male and female members within each academic rank) as well as participants' experiences within these departments (e.g., perceptions about the relationship between personal friendships, gender, age, power, resource distribution, etc.). I completed a social network analysis, followed by in-depth one-on-one interviews to gain a better understanding of how faculty members perceived their own identities, and how these identities shaped their interactions with colleagues, subsequently affording them (or limiting) their access to valued relationships and resources.

This study is an integrated analysis of data collected through online social network surveys and one-on-one interviews. For the first part of the study, participating faculty members completed an online network survey, through which they indicated which departmental colleagues they interacted with and for what purposes (e.g., help with research, help with teaching, general advice, friendship). Motivations behind interaction were determined by a list of questions adapted from Finkelstein's research about faculty colleagueship patterns (1982). For example, participants were asked to share their responses to questions such as "Who do you go to for help with teaching?" and "Who comes to you for help with research?"

Following completion of the social network survey, I conducted interviews to explore faculty members' behaviors in depth, and to give people the authority to express the salience of their own intersecting identities as they make sense of their personal experiences and interactions within social groups (McCall, 2005). Importantly, each interview protocol was individualized according to the nature of participants' demographic characteristics and departmental networks, which were self-reported through the surveys. Interviews included discussions of departmental culture, perceptions of self, similarities and differences in relation to colleagues,

NEW DIRECTIONS FOR INSTITUTIONAL RESEARCH • DOI: 10.1002/ir

nature and quality of relationships with colleagues, and related professional and personal experiences within the institution and academic departments.

Data Analysis. I analyzed the data in a sequential approach, which favored consideration of group composition (in this case, academic departments) as well as the layered meaning of identities (such as gender, race, age, nationality, marital status, and academic rank) that faculty members relied on to construct meaning of their experiences within their departments. In addition to the value they add to the richness of data and depth of analysis, each type of research complements the other. Network data were shared with participants during interviews and thus facilitated data collection about interaction within departments during individual interviews. Interviews generated data on the experiences of each participant, which contextualized and enriched analysis of survey data. (For more detailed information about the study, see Pifer, 2010.)

Individual Network Analysis. There were three stages of analysis in this study. First, I analyzed each participant's networks on the basis of his or her survey responses. Social network analysis was used to explore the questions of what networks existed within each department, the members within each network, and to a certain extent how members of the network interacted. This process allowed identification of themes, patterns, isolates (colleagues with whom participants indicated no interaction), and other characteristics that contributed to my understanding of each person's interactions with departmental colleagues.

I included the results of the social network analysis in a summary report, which was then shared and discussed with participants during the interviews. The summary reports contained sociograms—images of each faculty member's network of relationships according to the categories of collegial interaction suggested by Finkelstein (1982). A sample report is included as Figure 3.1; circles represent female colleagues and squares represent male colleagues. This image depicts the networks of one participant, Scott, who was an assistant professor in the Business Department.

This summary image highlights certain patterns in, and characteristics of, Scott's network. For example, he indicated that he interacts with about one-third of the fifteen tenure-track faculty members in the Business Department. Within his network of relationships in the department, he seems to reach out to the same group of five or six people and reported no connections to the remainder of his departmental colleagues. Certain people, like Hunter, show up in most or all of his function-specific networks, while Scott interacts with others, like Cindy, for only one or two purposes. Conceptualizing the survey data in these ways allows for an initial understanding of Scott's networking behaviors and experiences, and it sets the foundation for further analysis.

Qualitative Analysis. Analysis of each participant's social network was followed by interviews, during which participants' social networks and

Figure 3.1. Scott's Networks of Relationships

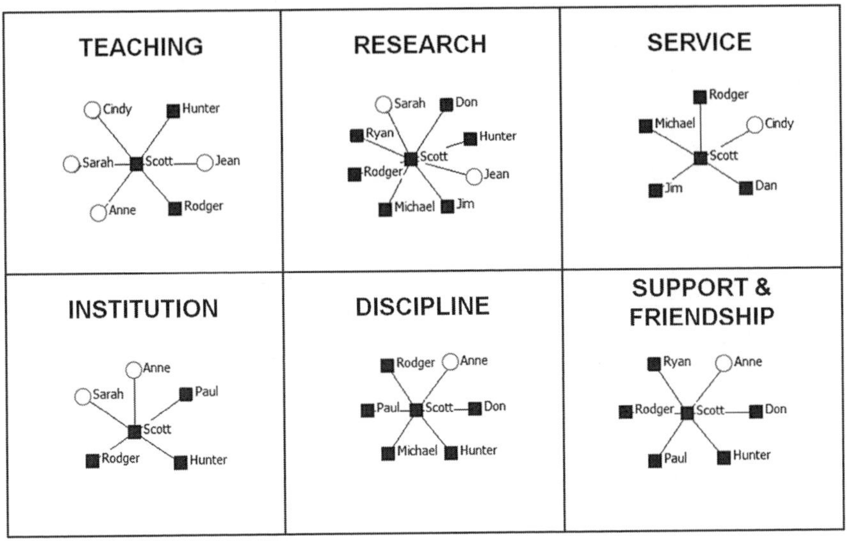

identity-based experiences within their departments were explored in greater depth. In the second stage of data analysis, interviews were transcribed verbatim, and emergent themes were identified, coded, and explored in depth. This included attention to how individual and institutional characteristics appeared to affect faculty members' experiences.

Departmental Network Analysis (Quantitative Analysis). For the third and final stage of data analysis, I returned to the network survey data to explore themes and compare experiences within each department. I used two network analysis measures to quantify the relationships between departmental colleagues. These included degree centrality and multiplexity. Both measures can be linked to the degree of access to network resources that a person has, the relative access to resources across network members, and patterns within and across identity-based characteristics.

Degree centrality is an indicator of how well connected someone is within a network. I calculated the centrality scores for each participant's network in general, as well as for the six function-specific networks. Centrality scores can be understood as the total number colleagues to whom participants indicated having a connection. The degree centrality scores of all participants are included as Table 3.1. There were fifteen tenured or tenure-track faculty members in the Business Department (BUS) and twenty-eight tenured or tenure-track faculty members in the Social and Behavioral Sciences Department (SBS).

Multiplexity is the extent to which two people are linked together by more than one relationship or connected by more than one purpose.

Table 3.1. Centrality Scores, All Participants

Name	Dept.	Overall Network	Teaching Network	Research Network	Institutional Linkage	Disciplinary Linkage	Support and Friendship	Committees and Service
Amanda	SBS	17	3	8	8	3	6	5
Beth	SBS	11	3	3	6	1	9	1
Bill	SBS	18	2	3	7	13	6	11
Brad	BUS	11	5	3	1	4	8	5
David	SBS	15	3	8	4	12	13	4
Don	BUS	14	6	7	14	10	9	6
Jean	BUS	15	3	1	3	3	12	11
Jim	BUS	7	0	5	0	2	4	0
Justin	SBS	28	11	3	28	9	17	11
Kyle	BUS	5	4	4	0	0	3	0
Liam	SBS	20	3	13	14	10	16	11
Mark	SBS	36	8	13	36	8	26	1
Matthew	SBS	11	5	2	8	4	6	2
Michael	BUS	14	7	9	10	8	12	13
Mollie	SBS	17	6	9	8	11	7	0
Nicole	SBS	14	3	5	5	3	6	0
Rodger	BUS	20	1	6	20	8	19	20
Ryan	BUS	15	4	11	8	5	9	15
Sarah	BUS	18	6	6	12	12	10	15
Scott	BUS	15	6	10	6	6	7	7
Sidney	BUS	19	9	10	14	10	11	10

Multiplexity scores can be understood as the total number of purposes that are met within a relationship between two people (for example, the tie between two faculty members who conduct research together, co-teach a course, and socialize together outside of work would have a centrality score of 3). Multiplexities may be more common between people who perceive themselves to be similar to others than between those who do not identify with others as closely. The multiplex scores between participants are included as Table 3.2 (Business Department) and Table 3.3 (Social and Behavioral Sciences Department).

Table 3.2. Multiplexity of Ties, Business Department

	Brad	Don	Jean	Jim	Kyle	Michael	Rodger	Ryan	Sarah	Scott	Sidney
Brad	—	*	1	*	1	1	4	5	1	2	5
Don	1	—	*	*	5	1	4	1	1	5	3
Jean	2	1	—	1	2	6	4	1	6	2	2
Jim	*	*	*	—	2	*	*	*	*	2	*
Kyle	*	*	*	*	—	2	*	3	*	*	2
Michael	5	6	6	2	6	—	4	5	2	6	3
Rodger	4	3	4	3	5	4	—	4	6	4	5
Ryan	4	4	1	2	6	6	3	—	3	2	6
Sarah	1	*	6	1	4	3	6	3	—	4	5
Scott	*	3	2	2	*	3	6	2	4	—	*
Sidney	4	2	1	2	5	3	6	5	6	*	—

Note: * Indicates no tie between participants.

Table 3.3. Multiplexity of Ties, Social and Behavioral Sciences Department

	Amanda	Beth	Bill	David	Justin	Liam	Mark	Matthew	Mollie	Nicole
Amanda	—	2	1	*	4	3	3	2	*	3
Beth	1	—	*	4	2	3	2	1	*	1
Bill	1	*	—	*	3	1	3	2	*	1
David	*	3	*	—	5	*	4	1	*	*
Justin	5	4	4	5	—	3	4	2	1	3
Liam	4	5	2	*	4	—	4	3	*	3
Mark	4	4	1	2	3	5	—	3	2	5
Matthew	1	1	*	*	3	2	3	—	*	*
Mollie	2	1	1	2	1	1	5	2	—	3
Nicole	2	2	*	*	1	3	4	*	1	—

Note: * Indicates no tie between participants.

Emerging Intersectionality

Findings demonstrated the importance of participants' multiple and intersecting identities in shaping their experiences and relationships within their departments, as well as the subsequent exchange of resources such as advice, research collaboration, friendship, leadership and administrative opportunities, and reductions in teaching loads. Findings also suggest four areas in which research such as this may be beneficial for institutional research about intersectionality in the faculty experience, and relevant connections to institutional outcomes: faculty reflections about identity, member checking and interpretation, unanticipated responses, and comparative analysis.

Faculty Reflections About Identity. One benefit of this mixed-methods approach was the opportunity for participants to engage in a more comprehensive process of reflection, fostering a deeper understanding of their identities and experiences. Beginning such work with collection and analysis of social network data allowed participants to quantify and conceptualize their relationships meaningfully. For example, Amanda was an assistant professor in the Social and Behavioral Sciences Department. During her interview, she indicated she had spent time thinking about her experiences and relationships after completing the network survey. She was curious about my interpretation of her survey responses, and eager to explain her experiences and relationships in greater detail as we reviewed the results of the network analysis together. As we spoke, she expressed a variety of concerns relating to various dimensions of her identity. She worried about being the only pre-tenure faculty member in her department after a series of unsuccessful tenure bids in recent years. Her identity as an interdisciplinary researcher was quite salient and important to her; she interacted more with colleagues in one of the university's research centers than with the faculty in her academic department and wondered about the implications of these relationships. She was pregnant and had a young child, and her identity as a mother left her worried about trying to maintain her scholarly productivity, while also remaining committed to her family and her husband's career goals. Further, she expressed feeling socially disengaged from departmental colleagues because of her parenting responsibilities.

Amanda's experience highlights the intersections of her personal and professional identities as they related to her work. Her case also illustrates what makes this approach particularly intriguing: her thoughtful and detailed accounts of her experiences at the university resulted from the multistage process of completing the survey, contemplating her experiences independently, and making sense of them while describing them in great detail during her interview and discussion of her departmental network. This mixed-methods approach gives faculty participants opportunities to explore and express intersecting identities and institutional experiences. As institutional researchers obtain data from faculty members for their own purposes, they also give participating faculty a chance to reflect on, and perhaps change, their professional behaviors and experiences. Just as researchers may use this approach to improve faculty experiences on their campuses, the process may result in an awareness that enables faculty members to enact positive change in their career as well.

Member-Checking and Interpretation. Another advantage to this integration of social network analysis and qualitative inquiry is the opportunity for the researcher to obtain clarification or greater explanation about participants' identities and identity-based perceptions. For example, Scott was a single, white assistant professor in the Business Department who immigrated to the United States for his career. His survey responses indicated that network connections to his male colleagues afforded access to support with writing, research collaborations, and introductions to influential scholars. His connections to female colleagues in the department, however, were primarily for teaching-related purposes (see Figure 3.1). In other words, the quantified measures of Scott's relationships highlighted some interesting points for additional qualitative investigation.

When asked about his teaching network during his interview, Scott pointed to the various ways in which he formed relationships with colleagues: "Well, first, you have the formal aspect of it. Senior faculty members need to sit in junior faculty members' classes and give feedback." He noted that Rodger was included in his teaching network because of his role as department chair. In addition to these formal causes for interaction, Scott described informal prompts, such as colleagues who were "really nice" and those who had reached out to discuss teaching with him. These colleagues were all women. He explained, "usually the women have a much better intuition for teaching so I talk to them [for that purpose]."

Scott's opinion about the gender difference in his colleagues' teaching and research "intuitions" has implications not only for his own experiences but also for those of his colleagues. Behaviors and assumptions like his reinforce stereotypes of female academics as being strong only in the teaching and mothering roles and exclude women from opportunities to cultivate their identities as researchers, influential members of scholarly disciplines, and institutional leaders. Such findings about with whom faculty choose to interact, and why, can prompt researchers to explore the potential for the cumulative disadvantage or differential access to resources that results from identity-based interactions within institutional contexts.

Unanticipated Responses. Combining network surveys and interviews supports the emergence of unanticipated or previously unacknowledged intersections in faculty members' conceptualization of their identities and experiences. This was especially visible in Sarah's narrative. She was an associate professor in the Business Department. Her survey responses indicated she was professionally involved in her department in many ways, but she also perceived herself as dissimilar to her colleagues according to multiple personal characteristics. She explained that although she was a very accomplished scholar who enjoyed collaborating with and mentoring her colleagues, she experienced self-doubt and isolation as a single woman with no children in a department of mostly married, mostly male peers. When asked how she was different from her departmental colleagues, she replied, "certainly being single." She struggled to articulate how her relationships with colleagues were affected by her marital status: "I think that it's—I don't know how to describe that, because I feel like—I feel that whole spousal issue. . . . You know, I'm the odd duck. That's fine. But it's easier for me to connect with people who don't have all of that built-in stuff." Personally, she recalled incidents such as the time her department chair tried to set her up on a date with someone, and how she struggled to find peers her age who did not have child care responsibilities. Professionally, she expressed concern that she was expected to be more available for departmental service and committee work than her married colleagues and those with children.

Relying exclusively on Sarah's degree centrality and multiplexity scores, one might conclude that she was highly connected within the Business Department; yet in her interview Sarah expressed unanticipated concerns about her career. It was not exclusively age, gender, marital status, career stage, or lack of children that defined her experience. Rather, her identity was shaped by the intersection of her roles as a middle-aged, mid-career, single, childless woman within a competitive academic environment. Her experience permits insight into how personal components of faculty members' identities emerge as meaningful in professional contexts. Sarah's perceived lack of fit and self-doubt, despite her professional status as a tenured faculty member in a highly regarded department and institution, remind us of the importance of considering layered identities when researching faculty members' experiences on campus.

Comparative Analysis. Combining network research and interviews fosters comparative exploration of multiple participants' perceptions of and experiences within the same institutional contexts. The experiences of two participants in the Social and Behavioral Sciences Department illustrate how this approach can shed light on disparity between faculty members' institution-based experiences. Bill was a white, tenured, full professor in his sixties who was married and had adult children. He was a former dean in the college and had been at the institution for several decades. Nicole was a Latina, untenured, assistant professor in her thirties. She had moved far from her family to accept her position, and she did not have a partner or children. According to Bill's and Nicole's survey data, both participants seemed to form friendships and supportive relationships with peers who were similar to them in rank and age.

When asked if rank affected faculty members' interactions, Bill replied, "No and as a matter of fact, we've made deliberate attempts to not segregate faculty by rank. And I refuse to have separate meetings with full professors and assistant professors." Nicole's experiences were quite different, however. In her interview, she declared, "One thing I know for sure—men and women are approached very differently in the classroom. You get an older white male into the classroom, students take him more seriously. A young female will not be taken that seriously." She stated that if she could, she would change the culture of her department and institution so that people would "acknowledge" and "talk about" her concerns. Nicole struggled to make sense of her experiences in an environment in which "there was yet for someone to admit there is a difference" in faculty members' experiences. She went on to describe how elements of her personal identity affected how her students, her colleagues, and administrators treated her. She was frustrated by her experiences and concerned about her ability to earn tenure in the department and institution. These perceptions, and subsequent fears about her career success, affected her interactions within the department. As she said, "I'm very careful about who I talk to about [my concerns] because, again, it's the ideology that if you're a certain gender and a certain age, you're automatically good. But in my informal networks, I talk about this issue."

Through language such as "we" and "I refuse," Bill's responses suggest his position of power and his perception of himself as an integral member of the department. He was quick to refute the possibility of rank-based differences, and possibly protective of the institution and department where he had served for so long. Nicole, on the other hand, positioned herself as an outsider who worried that "they"—her older, tenured, white, male colleagues—would not hear her concerns. By comparing the networks and perceptions of Bill and Nicole, we can see how faculty members draw on their intersecting roles and identities to describe very different experiences within the same institutional, and even departmental, context.

The emergence of such findings is likely to be as informative to department members and campus leaders as it is to institutional researchers. For example, Bill joined the department at its inception and indicated that he worked hard to protect the rights of all faculty and to foster a positive working environment. As he said, "I was brought here to help build a college. And for the first dozen years of my career, I spent most of my time building a first-rate department." He probably would have been surprised and disappointed to learn of Nicole's frustrations. From Nicole's point of view, however, colleagues like Bill had not shown an interest in supporting her. Research such as this may furnish faculty members and administrators with an indirect yet powerful way of learning about and improving colleagues' experiences.

Intersectionality and Institutional Research

One challenge of conducting institutional research about faculty members' perceptions and experiences is that of connecting data to the fluid and intangible concept of identity. How faculty members perceive their own identities, particularly in relation to their colleagues and their professional experiences, is a unique and personal process. For example, one woman felt excluded from her departmental network because she was pregnant and caring for small children; another felt excluded because she did not have children. What isolated one faculty member was exactly what another perceived as a desirable trait that was missing from her own networking opportunities. A mixed-methods approach that relies on network data and interviews allows researchers to learn more about the relationships that exist between colleagues, and how faculty members perceive themselves in relation to their institutions, departments, and colleagues as well as how such perceptions affect their career success and satisfaction.

Several implications for intersectionality research arose from this study. Research about the experiences of groups and individuals within organizational contexts can positively influence policy development, operational procedures, and interpersonal relationships (Hancock, 2007b). By engaging in this type of inquiry, researchers can seek answers to questions about the faculty career as they relate specifically to their institutions and faculty members. For example, what personal characteristics and identities influence the experiences of female faculty in the STEM disciplines on campus? Are pre-tenure men of color with child care responsibilities connected to the same mentoring, support networks, and campus resources as their white or female peers? How do faculty members rely on their multidimensional sense of personal identity to make sense of their teaching and classroom experiences? These questions and others can be explored through a mixed-methods approach to intersectionality that allows institutional researchers to understand faculty members' experiences in context, and subsequently to improve policies and practices related to faculty careers at their institutions. Linking intersectionality to institutional outcomes such as retention, productivity, faculty satisfaction, recruitment strategies, tenure and promotion processes, and faculty rewards systems can help institutional researchers improve their understanding of the reciprocal relationship between individual career experiences and institutional success.

Network data about faculty members' connectedness to others, centrality or isolation within institutional networks, and participation in or exclusion from identity-based subgroups can supply researchers with otherwise unavailable insights about the relationship between identity and professional experiences. Qualitative interviews can explore faculty members' experiences, identities, perceptions, and relationships—and relevant outcomes of interest—in greater depth. Combining these two types of research can help identify opportunities to improve institutional cultures, policies, and practices as they relate to recruitment, support, and retention of faculty members representing all backgrounds and characteristics.

Identity is socially constructed through social, historical, political, and cultural influences (Abes, Jones, and McEwen, 2007; McCall, 2005).

NEW DIRECTIONS FOR INSTITUTIONAL RESEARCH • DOI: 10.1002/ir

People develop their identities (and their perceptions of the identities of others) on the basis of membership in particular social categories, and the meaning attributed to those categories (Shields, 2008). In institutional contexts, we incorporate personal and professional categories, as well as individual and institutional characteristics, into the construction of identity. These identities can be simple or complex. For example, we may identify someone as a historian, or as a tenured white female faculty member from Europe who has a prestigious grant, a partner who is on the tenure track, and caregiving responsibilities for an elderly parent. The more richly we allow ourselves to conceptualize faculty members' identities, the more deeply we may be able to understand how intersecting roles affect their relationships and experiences within institutional contexts, and the better equipped we will be to improve outcomes at both the individual and the institutional levels.

References

Abes, E. S., Jones, S. R., and McEwen, M. K. "Reconceptualizing the Model of Multiple Dimensions of Identity: The Role of Meaning-Making Capacity in the Construction of Multiple Identities." *Journal of College Student Development*, 2007, 48(1), 1–22.

Bowleg, L. "When Black + Lesbian + Woman ≠ Black Lesbian Woman: The Methodological Challenge of Qualitative and Quantitative Intersectionality Research." *Sex Roles*, 2008, 59, 312–325.

Brass, D.J., Galaskiewicz, J., Greve, H.R., and Tsai, W. "Taking Stock of Networks and Organizations: A Multilevel Perspective." *Academy of Management*, 2004, 47(6), 795–817.

Crenshaw, K. "Mapping the Margins: Intersectionality, Identity Politics, and Violence Against Women of Color." *Stanford Law Review*, 1991, 3(6), 1241–1299.

Di Leo, J. R. *Affiliations: Identity in Academic Culture*. Lincoln, NE: University of Nebraska Press, 2003.

Finkelstein, M. J. *Faculty Colleagueship Patterns and Research Productivity*. Paper presented at annual meeting of the American Educational Research Association. New York, April 1982.

Fitts, M. "Institutionalizing Intersectionality: Reflections on the Structure of Women's Studies Departments and Programs." In M. T. Berger and K. Guidroz (eds.), *The Intersectional Approach: Transforming the Academy Through Race, Class, and Gender*. Chapel Hill: University of North Carolina Press, 2009.

Griffin, K. A., Pifer, M. J., Humphrey, J. R., and Hazelwood, A. M. "(Re)Defining Departure: Exploring Black Professors' Experiences with and Responses to Racism and Racial Climate." *American Journal of Education*, 2011, 117(4), 495–526.

Hancock, A. "Intersectionality as a Normative and Empirical Paradigm." *Politics and Gender*, 2007a, 3(2), 248–254.

Hancock, A. "When Multiplication Doesn't Equal Quick Addition: Examining Intersectionality as a Research paradigm." *Perspectives on Politics*, 2007b, 5(1), 63–79.

Howard, R. D. *Using Mixed-Methods in Institutional Research*. Tallahassee, Fla.: Association for Institutional Research, 2007.

Ibarra, H. "Personal Networks of Women and Minorities in Management: A Conceptual Framework." *Academy of Management Review*, 1993, 18(1), 56–87.

Lester, J. "Performing Gender in the Workplace: Gender Socialization, Power, and Identity Among Women Faculty Members." *Community College Review*, 2008, 35(4), 277–305.

McCall, L. "The Complexity of Intersectionality." *Signs: Journal of Women in Culture and Society*, 2005, *30*(3), 1771–1800.

Peluchette, J.V.E. "Subjective Career Success: The Influence of Individual Difference, Family, and Organizational Variables. *Journal of Vocational Behavior,* 1993, *43*(2), 198–208.

Perry, G. K. "Exploring Occupational Stereotyping in the New Economy: The Intersectional Tradition Meets Mixed-methods Research." In M. T. Berger and K. Guidroz (eds.), *The Intersectional Approach: Transforming the Academy Through Race, Class, and Gender.* Chapel Hill: University of North Carolina Press, 2009.

Pifer, M. J. "Such a Dirty Word: Networks and Networking in Academic Departments." Unpublished doctoral dissertation, College of Education, Pennsylvania State University, 2010.

Poole, M., and Bornholt, L. "Career Development of Academics: Cross-Cultural and Lifespan Factors." *International Journal of Behavioral Development*, 1998, *22*(1), 103–126.

Shields, S. "Gender: An Intersectional Perspective." *Sex Roles*, 2008, *59*, 301–311.

Torres, V., Jones, S. R., and Renn, K. A. "Identity Development Theories in Student Affairs: Origins, Current Status, and New Approaches." *Journal of College Student Development*, 2009, *50*(6), 577–596.

Warner, L. R. "A Best Practices Guide to Intersectional Approaches in Psychological Research." *Sex Roles*, 2008, *59*, 454–463.

MEGHAN J. PIFER *is an assistant professor of education at Widener University.*

4

Focusing on the intersection of gender and racial identity, this chapter explores the utility of mixed methods to promote understanding of how black faculty experience cultural taxation, or the "black tax," in the academy.

Analyzing Gender Differences in Black Faculty Marginalization Through a Sequential Mixed-Methods Design

Kimberly A. Griffin, Jessica C. Bennett, Jessica Harris

The Civil Rights Movement and resulting influx of black undergraduates led to increased attention to and hiring of black scholars at predominantly white institutions (PWIs), where few to no black professors had ever been employed previously. Although many black faculty welcomed the opportunity to work at these campuses because it allowed them to focus more directly on their research, other students, administrators, and faculty at PWIs had a different set of plans and expectations. Specifically, black faculty were expected to engage in service in ways that their white colleagues were not, by mentoring black students, serving on diversity committees, and helping the institution navigate challenging issues with racism and discrimination (Banks, 1984).

In many ways, these expectations have not really changed. Several scholars have addressed the responsibilities that faculty colleagues and students may place on the shoulders of black professors, requiring a significant level of engagement in service from those black faculty members (e.g., Antonio, 2003; Tierney and Bensimon, 1996; Turner, Gonzalez, and Wood, 2008). Padilla (1994) refers to this phenomenon as "cultural taxation," which he specifically defined as the expectations that faculty of color are obligated to participate in departmental and institutional affairs concerning race and diversity. In considering the cultural taxation experiences of black faculty within the academy, Brayboy (2003) refers to "hidden service agendas" (p. 75) that include requirements to serve as the token voice of color or the fixer of problems related to race and ethnicity and take

NEW DIRECTIONS FOR INSTITUTIONAL RESEARCH, no. 151, Fall 2011 © Wiley Periodicals, Inc.
Published online in Wiley Online Library (wileyonlinelibrary.com) • DOI: 10.1002/ir.398

primary responsibility for teaching diversity courses. Students of color also often have high expectations, seeking black faculty as advisors and mentors who understand their unique experiences as people of color in higher education (Menges and Exum, 1983; Tierney and Bensimon, 1996).

Institutions that seek to recruit, retain, and promote faculty of color would be better positioned to do so if they attained a more nuanced understanding of how faculty of color spend their time and how that activity shapes the experiences of those faculty members. For example, even though engaging in service is consistent with the interests and cultural commitments of faculty of color in many cases (Baez, 2000), high expectations and subsequent level of involvement in service have the potential to present problems. Tenure and promotion decisions are primarily based on scholarly productivity, particularly at research universities. Commitments that draw faculty time away from research can be detrimental, and faculty of color are required to demonstrate the same rate of scholarly productivity regardless of their engagement in service activities (Padilla, 1994; Tierney and Bensimon, 1996). Thus, understanding high service expectations and commitments as a "tax," an extra time commitment that must be paid on top of other responsibilities, is an appropriate analogy in many ways.

Cultural taxation has been largely linked to service, but Joseph and Hirschfield (2010) suggest that cultural taxation should include *any* extra burdens faculty of color experience because of their race or ethnicity, acknowledging the problematic ways in which colleagues can question the abilities of faculty of color as scholars. African American faculty often face white peers' assumptions that they were hired for affirmative action purposes alone and are assumed to be less qualified scholars (Joseph and Hirschfield, 2010; Stanley, 2006; Turner, Gonzalez, and Wood, 2008). They may also face questions about the relevance and importance of race-related work, questioning its rigor, importance, and place within more "mainstream" academic work (Johnsrud and Sadao, 1998; Joseph and Hirschfield, 2010; Menges and Exum, 1983). Questions about their abilities and legitimacy may lead faculty to engage in a "proving process," by which black faculty work doubly hard to prove their worth and abilities as scholars and that they are deserving of their appointments and promotions (Banks, 1984; Johnsrud and Sadao, 1998; Joseph and Hirschfield, 2010; Menges and Exum, 1983; Stanley, 2006). For the purposes of this chapter, we embrace this expanded understanding of cultural taxation, integrating high service expectations and low academic expectations.

Using Mono-Method and Mixed-Methods Designs to Study Cultural Taxation

The nature and complexity of these issues limits the utility of mono-method studies of faculty experiences with cultural taxation. Surveys are efficient for studying large groups of people, testing hypotheses about phenomena, and developing findings that can be generalized; however, quantitative analyses are limited in depth and insight (Johnson and Onwuegbuzie, 2004), which are necessary to truly understand the comprehensive experiences and subsequent responses of black scholars. Thus survey analysis can give some insight to the frequency with which faculty encounter cultural taxation, but capturing the nature of these extra burdens and how faculty respond to them requires institutional researchers to use qualitative strategies. Qualitative methods alone may also be problematic because they do not supply institutional researchers and leaders with the information they might want or need to determine the prevalence of cultural taxation on their campuses or determine whether they are more frequently encountered in some departments than in others.

In the remainder of this chapter, we demonstrate how researchers can integrate qualitative and quantitative methods to gain a deeper understanding of the prevalence and nature of cultural taxation among black professors. In doing so, we show how the impact of cultural taxation on the experiences of black faculty in the academy is best captured using both quantitative and qualitative methods—allowing researchers to generate a picture of how faculty spend their time, how they characterize interactions within their institutions, and narratives of how these have an impact their experiences throughout their career.

We also explore how black male and female faculty experience cultural taxation in higher education differently. Despite the increased attention and discussion of the similar ways in which high service expectations, discrimination, and challenging campus environments negatively influence the salary, satisfaction, productivity, and opportunities for professional advancement for people of color and women in academia, little scholarly research explores how race and gender can simultaneously shape professors' experiences and outcomes. Men and women of color differ in their experience of colleagues' expectations and racism (Smith, Allen, and Danley, 2007; Washington and Newman, 1991). Further, faculty narratives and research on women of color suggest sexism creates a unique experience for women of color in the academy (Collins, 1998; Crenshaw, 1991; Gregory, 2001; Harley, 2008).

A Mixed-Methods Study of Black Faculty

In this section, we offer an example of a mixed-methods inquiry aimed at understanding black professors' experiences with cultural taxation. Both qualitative and quantitative data are disaggregated by gender to address the intersection of faculty identities, more fully exploring the ways in which black male and female faculty experience cultural taxation and a full range of expectations surrounding their roles and work in academia.

The Quantitative Survey. The survey data were collected by the Higher Education Research Institute (HERI) and were used to gain broad understanding of black faculty experiences with various forms of cultural taxation. For the current study, data from African American respondents to the 2004 Faculty Survey who were employed at research universities were analyzed (*n* = 500, fifty-nine institutions). Black men outnumber women (male = 53.5 percent, female = 46.5 percent) in the sample, and participants' ages ranged from under thirty to over seventy years old, with the average respondent being between forty-five and fifty-four. Fifty-four percent (*n* = 270) of participants had already received tenure, and another 28.4 percent (*n* = 142) were in tenure-track positions. Approximately one-quarter (24.8 percent, *n* = 124) of survey respondents were full professors, 34.6 percent (*n* = 173) were associate professors, 30.6 percent (*n* = 153) were assistant professors, and 9.8 percent (*n* = 49) were lecturers or instructors or had other academic designations. No professors were working at campuses designated as Hispanic Serving Institutions (HSIs), and 10.6 percent (*n* = 53) were employed at Historically Black Colleges and Universities (HBCUs). At the time of this survey, no Asian American Native American and Pacific Islander Serving Institutions (AANAPISIs) existed because this Minority Serving Institution category was not institutionalized until 2007.

The Qualitative Interviews. We constructed the qualitative dataset through a series of interviews conducted with twenty-eight black professors employed at two public, predominantly white, research universities of similar size and academic mission: Oceanside and Column Universities (pseudonyms). Seventeen Oceanside (ten males, seven females) and eleven Column professors (six males, five females) agreed to participate in this study. Participants had been professors for an average of sixteen years. Five participants were assistant professors, eleven associate professors, and twelve full professors at the time of interview. Participants engaged in sixty- to ninety-minute interviews, during which they were asked to describe their academic experiences throughout their careers, particularly during their time at the current institution. In addition to discussing their mentoring relationships with students (the core focus of the larger study), faculty were asked to reflect more generally on their engagement in service, the nature of interactions with colleagues, and perceptions of colleagues' expectations and perceptions of their work.

Together, the qualitative and quantitative analyses deepened our understanding of how black faculty perceive their distinctive experiences in higher education, as well as differences in black male and female faculty perspectives. This study can be best described as a sequential design, where one form of data analysis is conducted first to inform a complementary analysis of the other (Creswell and Plano Clark, 2007). Sequential analyses can be QUAN-QUAL, or a quantitative analysis that is expanded by qualitative strategies, or QUAL-QUAN, where the qualitative data informed development of a survey instrument or analysis of a quantitative dataset. This research was conducted as a QUAL-QUAN study, where

NEW DIRECTIONS FOR INSTITUTIONAL RESEARCH • DOI: 10.1002/ir

qualitative analysis informed an analysis of faculty responses to specific questions on the HERI faculty survey. In many ways, however, this study was conducted as a QUAL-QUAN-QUAL analysis. Emerging themes from the qualitative data informed the selection and exploration of variables for comparison in a national dataset, which was followed by a more focused and detailed analysis of the qualitative data to triangulate and permit deeper understanding of the quantitative findings.

First, the interview transcripts were reviewed to identify the key themes in the experiences of black professors emerging from the data. Each researcher read all of the transcripts from female professors, wrote a memo on the emerging findings, and then repeated this process for black male professors.

The team then met to discuss the themes that were consistent across the interviews, as well as experiences and concerns that appeared more salient for men as compared to women, and vice versa.

The preliminary qualitative analyses directed the analysis of HERI Faculty Survey data, largely composed of calculating descriptive statistics and t-tests. Responses to HERI Survey questions representing issues high-lighted within the qualitative interviews and the larger scholarly literature (e.g., commitment to service, low expectations from colleagues, and per-ceptions about the need to work hard to disprove stereotypes) were ana-lyzed first, comparing the responses of black men and women. Subsequent analyses focusing on the amount of stress these activities cause, which were also disaggregated by gender, were included to better capture the potential influence of these experiences (see Table 4.1 for variable values).

In the third step, the quantitative findings were compared to the emerging themes as a means of triangulating and yielding a more nuanced understanding of the qualitative data. Differences illuminated in the quan-titative data were revisited and explored in the qualitative data with more detail and precision. Qualitative data were coded through deductive and inductive processes. Consistent with methods outlined by Bogdan and Biklen (1998) and Merriam (1998), we then reread, coded, and organized the data using ATLAS.ti software. Themes with similar underlying princi-ples were clustered together, compared to early perceptions of emerging themes, and developed into reports of the experiences of black male and female faculty.

Findings of the Mixed-Methods Inquiry

This study adopts the broad definition of cultural taxation to explore the experiences of black faculty, integrating these ideas into the construct of the "black tax." As noted above, our understanding of the "black tax" incorporates both the higher service expectations and lowered aca-demic expectations of cultural taxation for faculty of color (Joseph and Hirschfield, 2010; Padilla, 1994). Although a familiar term used in

Table 4.1. 2004 HERI Faculty Survey Variables in Quantitative Analysis

Question	Variable Values
During the present term, how many hours per week on the average do you actually spend on each of the following activities: Hours per week advising/counseling students Hours per week in committees/meetings Hours per week spent on community/public service	1 = None; 2 = 1–4 hours; 3 = 5–8 hours; 4 = 9–12 hours; 5 = 13–16 hours; 6 = 17–20 hours; 7 = 21–34 hours; 8 = 35–44 hours; 9 = 45 hours or more
Please indicate the extent to which each of the following has been a source of stress for you over the last two years: The promotion process Subtle discrimination Self-imposed expectations Committee work Faculty meetings	1= Not at all; 2 = Somewhat; 3 = Extensive
Please indicate the extent to which you: Have to work harder to be perceived as a legitimate scholar	1 = Not at all; 2 = To some extent; 3 = To great extent
Indicate the extent to which you agree or disagree with the following statements: My research is valued by faculty in my department My teaching is valued by faculty in my department	1 = Disagree strongly; 2 = Disagree somewhat; 3 = Agree somewhat; 4 = Agree strongly

popular media, we draw this term from the actual participants in this study, who used it to describe their experiences in higher education. One male faculty member used this terminology in saying:

> I've talked to black faculty who say it's the "black tax" . . . being a black faculty member, there's a tax you have to pay—you've got to put in a little bit of extra time. And I think many of us feel OK with that because we know that we would not have been here were it not for some folks paying their "black tax" when we were graduate students.

Participants referenced the "black tax" throughout their narratives, placing a name on the added expectations of black faculty. As reflected in the quote above, many of the references to the "black tax" also indicate that this concept is shared and discussed by black faculty via cultural transmission, the passing of culturally relevant information from person to person.

Both black female and male faculty express experiencing the "black tax" throughout their narratives. For example, participants' narratives reflect the engagement in service observed among black faculty. As one black male faculty member said:

> They put you in every community across campus, so you end up doing more community service than your white colleagues and you don't get any credit for it. So you're setting them up to fail basically. . . .

This faculty member identifies the challenges that black faculty face in managing unwritten service-related expectations while simultaneously addressing the formal expectations associated with the tenure and promotion processes. This feeling of being "set up to fail" was articulated throughout the faculty narratives in terms of challenges to attaining tenure, personal and physical health costs, and overall stress associated with balancing service and research expectations.

Black faculty also addressed colleagues' perceptions of their place in their departments, institutions, and the academy. A black male faculty member described it in this way:

> You're very, very cautious about what you say. You tend to not speak your mind . . . because anything you'd have to say you would think may have racial consequences because you're the only racial minority. . . . You have to be twice as good as people who work in other areas and you have to publish in places that are twice as high and you have to do more of it.

This quote is reflective of a theme in the data, where faculty repeatedly expressed their perceived place within the academy. Their race is a constant marker undermining their ability to participate fully or without caution. In addition, many faculty appear to respond to their precarious positions by working twice as hard to ensure they are regarded as able scholars.

The quotes above broadly acknowledge how black faculty described experiencing the "black tax," but there were distinctions in how male and female faculty spoke about and responded to their experiences. The sections below highlight these differences, integrating an analysis of qualitative data with data collected from a national sample of black faculty participating in the 2004 HERI Faculty Survey data.

Gender Differences in Service Expectations. Analysis of black faculty responses to questions regarding service in the HERI Faculty Survey painted a picture regarding how black faculty experience high service expectations. On the basis of their responses to various questions, black male and female faculty members appear to spend similar amounts of time

Table 4.2. Gender Differences in Black Faculty Reports of Cultural Taxation

	Overall		Black Women		Black Men		
	Mean	SD	Mean	SD	Mean	SD	p
Hours per week advising/ counseling students	2.46	0.88	2.43	0.896	2.48	0.857	0.556
Hours per week in committees/meetings	2.39	0.976	2.36	0.968	2.42	0.985	0.56
Hours per week spent on community/public service	1.95	0.93	2.00	1.069	1.90	0.792	0.297
Stress experienced because of committee work	1.70	0.697	1.78	0.750	1.63	0.641	0.016
Stress experienced because of faculty meetings	1.69	0.711	1.81	0.756	1.58	0.654	0.000

engaging in activities that are considered faculty service. In other words, there were no statistically significant differences in the average number of hours each week black male and female faculty spent advising and counseling students (male x = 2.48, female x = 2.43, p = .556), engaging in committee work and meetings (male x = 2.42, female x = 2.36, p = .56), and participating in community and/or public service (male x = 1.90, female x = 2.00, p = .297; see Table 4.2).

Despite similar time commitments, women appear to have different experiences from their male counterparts when engaged in these activities. Women were more likely than men to report faculty meetings (women x = 1.81, men x = 1.58, p = .000) and committee work (women x = 1.78, men x = 1.63, p = .016) were sources of stress in the past two years. The differences observed in reported stress levels point to potential differences in how black men and women view and experience service-related responsibilities. Qualitative analyses of data collected from faculty at Oceanside and Column Universities allows exploration of these differences, suggesting that how black female faculty engage in service is indeed distinctive from black men.

For example, when speaking about interacting with students, women were more likely to report offering both academic and personal support. One female faculty member encapsulated the difference between how male and female faculty interacted with students:

> I mean, I do think that women faculty in general and women of color are more likely to get sucked into the lives of students in a way that I'm just not sure that male faculty members do . . . sometimes I just have way too much personal knowledge about situations . . . you're expected to be nurturing.

By highlighting the differences in expectations and behavior between men and women, this female faculty member articulates gender differences in the form, rather than frequency, of faculty-student interactions. In addition to these personal perceptions of differences, this faculty member, perhaps more strikingly, identifies others' expectations of her role in the academy. These expectations may reflect not only a level of commitment to working with students of color but also the particular role that black women are expected to play as the caretakers of students and junior colleagues in the academy (Harley, 2008).

In contrast to the personal nature of the relationships this female faculty person and others described, most of the black male faculty discussed their relationships with students as staying within the parameters of academia. Some spoke of forming personal relationships with students, but many black male faculty more often identified the importance of maintaining appropriate boundaries with students and spoke of their relationships with students in purely academic terms. This can be seen in one male faculty member's critique of a colleague's mode of interacting with students: "I felt like he emphasized the personal relationship over the actual real mentoring in terms of preparing people for research and then helping them get jobs and helping them write." This faculty member clearly views developing close personal relationships as being in conflict with successful academic mentorship.

It is possible, and likely, that engaging in close advising relationships that incorporate personal and professional development is more stressful or occupies more of a faculty member's energy than those that are purely professional. If women are more likely to participate in these closer relationships, it may explain why we see little difference in time spent on service, but different levels of stress based partially in emotional investment.

Though not as clear as the differences observed with student advising, there appear to be some differences in how black male and female faculty experience service on committees. A few of the women spoke of the pressure and expectation to serve on committees—with one sharing that she serves on several committees because it was important to have issues relevant to African Americans voiced and represented: "If you don't accept [a committee appointment] then your viewpoint will not be represented. So it's a different level of pressure, I think, than the average professor faces." This sense of there being nobody else to perform the work was a common theme for female faculty service commitments—on committees or to students—that did not appear often in the male faculty perspectives and may be associated with increased stress in performing committee work. The male faculty also talked about working on committees, but they made fewer references to pressure. Rather, as one faculty member noted, they more often framed committee work as part of the standard cadre of work for black faculty: "We have all sorts of programs and events and alumni meetings and committee meetings. So there's a lot of citizenship work that you do . . . that's sort of standard." The reference to "standard" behavior may be seen as an expectation, but this faculty member did not explicitly identify any experiences of feeling pressured to serve. A few of the black male faculty explicitly used words such as "volunteer" and "voluntary" to describe service in advancement of racial issues, a distinct difference from women who used language such as "expectation" or "pressure" to describe their role in committee work.

Given the differences in the nature of their relationships with students and experiences with service on committees, it is not entirely surprising that the black female faculty spoke of a different kind of cost to themselves as they worked with students and engaged in other forms of service. Both male and female black faculty discussed the time cost of these commitments and the negative impact it could have on promotion and tenure, especially given that these processes focus more on scholarly productivity than service (Tierney and Bensimon, 1996). However, in addition to the challenges presented in terms of time, women more frequently identified personal costs, which also may afford some insight into differing levels of stress experienced due to service. For example, one female faculty member explained:

> Because it's so time-consuming and exhausting I probably have made some wrong choices. . . . I think, until this year I thought that I could do it all. That I just would work harder on the weekends or just stay up later at night and do my own [work].

This quote points to the high expectations that black female faculty place on themselves to do it all. This internalized expectation, in concert with the pressures of external expectations, may be contributing to the stress black female faculty experience. Other costs and possible areas of stress identified by women included failing health and challenges to family life, echoing Harley's articulation (2008) of the physical and psychological challenges faced by black female faculty.

The black male professors spoke with more frequency about the costs of engaging in service activities that had a direct impact on promotion and tenure. One male faculty member noted the high service loads placed on black faculty, and recommended the following:

> You have to learn to say no at least until you get your tenure because you get rewarded in academia by the number and the quality of the publications and not how much time you spend mentoring students.

This articulation of "saying no" is reflected in varying terms and degrees among the male narratives. Another black male professor indicated that getting to tenure would allow black faculty to "exert the kind of influence that I think many black academics need to have in order to make change on the university campus." This perspective speaks to a perception of service work that was somewhat different from what women shared; men described service as something to be deferred until their status at the institution is more secure. Although they acknowledged the stresses and strains of service, female faculty less often articulated their tendency to say no. As noted above, some openly acknowledged that they should be more mindful of their time, but they seemed to take on these additional responsibilities and less often articulated boundaries that resemble those of black male faculty.

Stereotypes and Expectations. From analysis of data from the HERI Faculty Survey, black faculty appear to experience subtle forms of discrimination, consistent with the literature on the experiences of faculty of color (Johnsrud and Sadao, 1998; Trower and Chait, 2002; Stanley, 2006; see Table 4.3). Whereas data suggest that black faculty encounter and experience stress because of subtle discrimination, black female faculty were more likely to report subtle discrimination was a source of stress than black men did (men x = 1.65, women x = 1.90, p = .000). Survey data also highlight the different ways in which black female and male faculty experience subtle discrimination. Black women were less likely to agree that colleagues in their department valued their research (men = 2.84, female = 2.67, p = .034) or teaching (men = 3.14, women = 2.91, p = .003) than male faculty.

Perhaps the gender differences in whether or not black faculty feel valued can be explained by the difference in how black male and female faculty encounter subtle discrimination on campus and in their departments. Analysis of interviews with black faculty offers insight into the

Table 4.3. Gender Differences in Black Faculty Reports of Expectations, Marginalization, and Proving Process Behaviors

	Overall		Black Women		Black Men		
	Mean	SD	Mean	SD	Mean	SD	p
Have to work harder to be perceived as a legitimate scholar	2.15	0.800	2.37	0.724	1.96	0.815	0.000
My research is valued by faculty in my department	2.76	0.902	2.67	0.950	2.84	0.853	0.034
My teaching is valued by faculty in my department	3.03	0.858	2.91	0.901	3.14	0.805	0.003
Stress experienced because of the promotion process	1.72	0.811	1.83	0.835	1.62	0.778	0.006
Stress experienced because of subtle discrimination	1.77	0.742	1.90	0.728	1.65	0.736	0.000
Stress experienced because of self-imposed expectations	2.08	0.762	2.19	0.735	1.97	0.770	0.001

nature of the subtle discrimination black faculty experience, and how that differs by gender. Black men speculated about the doubt surrounding their ability, while women more often recounted tangible and direct encounters with colleagues questioning their abilities. For example, a woman professor discussed her tenure process and describes her colleagues not looking at her as a "peer" until she received tenure. But even then, she noted her colleagues did not see her as "a peer comparable to them . . . wondering was I really good enough to be . . . their colleague." Similarly, another female professor described how a colleague expressed a lack of confidence in her work ethic and questioned her ability as a scholar, expressing his belief that she would be promoted because of her identity rather than the quality of her work: "I had one white guy say to me, 'Well, you'll do fine . . . basically, you don't really have to work that hard because you're a black woman. It's handed to you.'" In both of these quotes, the professors directly point to race and gender playing a part in how their abilities and ideas were judged within their respective departments. Black female faculty seemed to depict colleagues' doubt due not only to their race but also to their gender. These feelings of "double doubt" are the internalization and subsequent manifestation of double jeopardy in black female experiences (St. Jean and Feagin, 1998).

Black male faculty illustrated the perceived reservations of colleagues differently, describing a feeling of suspicion surrounding them at all times. For example, one black male professor described speculation from his colleagues surrounding the theoretical approach he took in his discipline. Yet he said the speculation was not openly communicated to him and was "just sort of like that discourse that you hear about." Several male faculty members described feeling as if someone was always watching them, resulting in the need to be constantly on guard. As one male faculty member explained:

> I think it's just healthy to always think you're being watched closely . . . that you don't have any privacy . . . you have to be on guard all the time. Because people are looking, I feel that people are looking at me through a different lens.

Black men expressed a feeling of being scrutinized at all times. However, their narratives did not describe as many encounters with colleagues who directly questioned their academic qualifications as black women.

From this qualitative analysis, we see women experiencing overt criticism from colleagues, who root their assumptions in beliefs about affirmative action in hiring, which cannot fully be traced back to race or gender alone. Men suspected that they were being watched closely, yet they offered fewer instances of their abilities being questioned in a direct way. These narratives give insight into the distinctions observed in the quantitative data, suggesting women's abilities in teaching and research may be critiqued more overtly than their male counterparts, resulting in a higher level of stress.

Responding to Doubts: The Proving Process. Similar to the "proving process" described in previous scholarship (Banks, 1984; Johnsrud and Sadao, 1998; Joseph and Hirschfield, 2010; Menges and Exum, 1983; Stanley, 2006), both black male and female faculty appear to react to the skepticism of their white colleagues by working twice as hard to prove themselves. However, similar to the trends described above, disaggregating our analysis of data from the HERI Faculty Survey revealed gender differences. Black women were more likely than black male professors to report they felt they had to work harder to be perceived as legitimate scholars (men $x = 1.96$, women $x = 2.37$, $p = .000$) and more likely to report that self-imposed expectations were a source of stress (men $x = 1.97$, women $x = 2.19$, $p = .001$; see Table 4.3).

The qualitative data collected from faculty at Oceanside and Column Universities yields some insights into these differences. Analyses suggest black male faculty members tend to view the proving process as just another part of the job. For example, one black male professor noted, "You can't avoid it [working twice as hard], and you're expected to do things and you sort of have to because there's nobody else to do it." Similar to trends observed in the qualitative dataset in discussions of service obligations, black male faculty members appear to describe the steps they take to prove themselves capable as commonplace and something that comes with the job. Interestingly, our qualitative data did not offer significant insight into why black women reported more stress in expectations for self and working harder to validate their positions. Women did not address this topic in the same ways as men. However, future research could and should examine how and why women place additional stress and higher expectations on themselves in light of the doubts they face.

Implications for Institutional Research

In conclusion, we offer a few recommendations for institutions and institutional researchers concerned about black faculty experiences, satisfaction, productivity, retention, or success.

College Faculty Climate Data. Although more frequently studied in relation to the experiences of students of color, campus climate—or the attitudes, perceptions, and expectations within an institutional community around issues of race, ethnicity, and diversity—has an effect on the lives of faculty as well (Harper and Hurtado, 2007; Hurtado, Milem, Clayton-Pedersen, and Allen, 1999). Trower and Chait (2002), Antonio (2003), and others describe the campus climate for faculty from underrepresented groups as "chilly" and less than ideal, translating to a lower rate of professional advancement, higher level of dissatisfaction, and a lower likelihood of retention. Thus we strongly recommend that institutions not forget to regularly collect data from faculty when assessing whether a campus environment is hospitable or welcoming for people from marginalized groups.

Consider National Datasets. In addition to conducting local campus assessments, this study suggests nationally administered datasets can also be a useful tool in gaining a deeper understanding of how black professors and others experience their environment. Using nationally administered surveys such as the HERI Faculty Survey can promote insights and contextual understanding of phenomena that shape the experiences of black male and female professors, imparting preliminary direction for investigation into issues that might be challenging for marginalized faculty at individual campuses.

Disaggregate by Race and Gender. The findings of this study also emphasize the importance of disaggregating data by race *and* gender to get a more detailed understanding of how the intersectionality of identities can shape professors' experiences. It is common practice to analyze the differences in experience or attitude between gender categories, racial/ethnic categories, or faculty rank when evaluating faculty experiences. These distinctions certainly will tell institutional researchers and their data constituents about the broad experiences of particular groups, and they can do much to meaningfully highlight disparities in experiences. However, recent literature (Collins, 1998; Crenshaw, 1991; Gregory, 2001; Harley, 2008; Smith, Allen, and Danley, 2007; Washington and Newman, 1991) and this study show that individuals do not experience their environments from the perspective of one identity at a time; in fact, these identities combine and interact. We argue that disaggregating data, or re-aggregating it, into different groupings of intersectional identities aids description of these differences and can be a powerful way to understand what is happening inside an institution and to direct further qualitative inquiry. This study also suggests there is great importance in being mindful of intersectionality when analyzing qualitative data. Rather than just reading and analyzing narratives of all participants at one institution or within one department—or even within one racial/ethnic group or gender—as a case, researchers would find great value in comparing narratives across multiple dimensions of identity.

Consider Utility of Qualitative Data. Consistent with the theme of this volume, the analyses of quantitative and qualitative data highlight the ways in which a mixed-methods analysis can inform conceptualizations of faculty experiences at the intersections of multiple identities. Although disaggregated analyses of quantitative data highlighted differences and distinctions between black male and female faculty experiences that might not be readily visible through traditional groupings, these analyses did not explain the reasons behind these distinctions. Using qualitative data in a targeted fashion was imperative to gain a better understanding of how the "black tax" was experienced differently by black male and female faculty, and it suggested possible reasons for the distinctions observed within the national quantitative sample participating in the HERI Faculty Survey. Qualitative methods can also be used to collect a more precise answer when quantitative questions have been misinterpreted or misunderstood by survey participants. For example, it is quite possible that men and women incorrectly estimate the amount of time devoted to work, and an underestimation of time spent working within the institution on the part of black women would offer one explanation as to why they reported more stress in committee work and faculty meetings. This shows that different interpretations of quantitative questions and their ensuing answers can result in incorrect and misleading data. With qualitative interviews, researchers are able to ask specific questions as to how one spends and classifies one's time on task, eliciting illustrative answers to questions.

Invest the Extra Effort. We acknowledge the challenges that using a mixed-methods approach, focusing on experiences situated in intersectionality, may entail. We think it is important and useful to disaggregate quantitative data when possible, but it should be noted that there are challenges to using quantitative data alone to assess effects between and among intersectional groups. The biggest challenge in disaggregating or re-aggregating data into groupings of identity, particularly at the institutional level, is that sample sizes may be too small from which to draw conclusions. National datasets and strategic use of disaggregation may minimize these challenges. Additionally, institutional researchers may find it time-consuming to engage participants in qualitative interviews, especially given other demands. Despite these challenges, we assert that mixed-method analyses that are mindful of the intersectionality of faculty identities will foster the most insightful and comprehensive understanding of their experiences with racism and sexism in the academy.

References

Antonio, A. L. "Diverse Student Bodies, Diverse Faculties." *Academe*, 2003, *89*(3), 14–17. Retrieved December 20, 2004, from http://www.aaup.org/AAUP/pubsres/academe/2003/ND/Feat/anto.htm.

Baez, B. "Race-Related Service and Faculty of Color: Conceptualizing Critical Agency in Academe." *Higher Education*, 2000, *39*, 363–391.

Banks, W. M. "Afro-American Scholars in the University." *American Behavioral Scientist*, 1984, *27*(3), 325–338.

Bogdan, R. C., and Biklen, S. K. *Qualitative Research in Education: An Introduction to Theory and Methods* (3rd ed.). Boston: Allyn and Bacon, 1998.

Brayboy, B.M.J. "The Implementation of Diversity in Predominantly White Colleges and Universities." *Journal of Black Studies*, 2003, *34*(1), 72–86.

Collins, P. H. "Intersections of Race, Class, Gender, and Nation: Some Implications for Black Family Studies." *Journal of Comparative Family Studies*, 1998, *29*(1), 27–36.

Crenshaw, K. "Mapping the Margins: Intersectionality, Identity Politics, and Violence Against Women of Color." *Stanford Law Review,* 1991, *43*(6), 1241–1299.

Creswell, J. W., and Plano Clark, V. L. *Designing and Conducting Mixed-Methods Research.* Thousand Oaks, Calif.: Sage, 2007.

Gregory, S. T. "Black Faculty Women in the Academy: History, Status, and Future." *Journal of Negro Education,* 2001, *70*(3), 124–138.

Harley, D. A. "Maids of Academe: African American Women Faculty at Predominantly White Institutions." *Journal of African American Studies,* 2008, *12*(1), 19–36.

Harper, S., and Hurtado, S. "Nine Themes in Campus Racial Climates and Implications for Institutional Transformation." In S. R. Harper and L. D. Patton (eds.), *Special Issue: Responding to the Realities of Race on Campus.* New Directions for Student Services, no. 120. San Francisco: Jossey-Bass, 2007.

Hurtado, S., Milem, J., Clayton-Pedersen, A., and Allen, W. R. "Enacting Diverse Learning Environments: Improving the Climate for Racial/Ethnic Diversity in Higher Education." *ASHE-ERIC Higher Education Report,* 1999, *26*(8), 1–116.

Johnson, R. B., and Onwuegbuzie, A. J. "Mixed-Methods Research: A Research Paradigm Whose Time Has Come." *Educational Researcher,* 2004, *33*(7), 14–26.

Johnsrud, L. K., and Sadao, K. C. "The Common Experience of 'Otherness': Ethnic and Racial Minority Faculty." *Review of Higher Education,* 1998, *21*(4), 315–342.

Joseph, T. D., and Hirschfield, L. E. "'Why Don't You Get Somebody New to Do It?' Race and Cultural Taxation in the Academy." *Ethnic and Racial Studies,* 2010, 1–21. Retrieved October 13, 2010, from http://www.informaworld.com/10.1080/01419870.2010.496489.

Menges, R. J., and Exum, W. H. "Barriers to the Progress of Women and Minority Faculty." *Journal of Higher Education,* 1983, *54*(2), 123–144.

Merriam, S. B. *Qualitative Research and Case Study Applications in Education.* San Francisco: Jossey-Bass, 1998.

Padilla, A. M. "Ethnic Minority Scholars, Research, and Mentoring: Current and Future Issues." *Educational Researcher,* 1994, *23*(4), 24–27.

St. Jean, Y., and Feagin, J. R. *Double Burden: Black Women and Everyday Racism.* Armonk, N.Y.: Sharpe, 1998.

Smith, W. A., Allen, W. R., and Danley, L. L. "'Assume the Position . . . You Fit the Description': Psychosocial Experiences and Racial Battle Fatigue Among African American Male College Students." *American Behavioral Scientist,* 2007, *51*(4), 551–578.

Stanley, C. A. "Coloring the Academic Landscape: Faculty of Color Breaking the Silence in Predominantly White Colleges and Universities." *American Educational Research Journal,* 2006, *43*(4), 701–736.

Tierney, W., and Bensimon, E. M. *Promotion and Tenure: Community and Socialization in Academe.* Albany: State University of New York Press, 1996.

Trower, C. A., and Chait, R. P. "Faculty Diversity: Too Little for Too Long." *Harvard Magazine,* 2002, *104*(4), 33–37, 98.

Turner, C.S.V., Gonzalez, J. C., and Wood, J. L. "Faculty of Color in Academe: What 20 Years of Literature Tells Us." *Journal of Diversity in Higher Education,* 2008, *1*(3), 139–168.

Washington, V., and Newman, J. "Setting Our Own Agenda: Exploring the Meaning of Gender Disparities Among Blacks in Higher Education." *Journal of Negro Education,* 1991, *60*(1), 19–35.

KIMBERLY A. GRIFFIN is an assistant professor of education policy studies at the Pennsylvania State University and a research associate in the Center for the Study of Higher Education.

JESSICA C. BENNETT is a doctoral student in Higher Education at the Pennsylvania State University.

JESSICA HARRIS is a doctoral student in higher education at the University of Denver.

5

In this chapter, the author discusses the utility of mixed-method approaches and intersectionality frameworks in analyzing and understanding inequities in college access faced by first-generation Asian American and Pacific Islander students.

An Introductory Mixed-Methods Intersectionality Analysis of College Access and Equity: An Examination of First-Generation Asian Americans and Pacific Islanders

Samuel D. Museus

It has now been almost half a century since the model minority myth—the stereotype that all Asian American and Pacific Islanders (AAPIs) achieve unparalleled and universal academic and occupational success—first emerged (Museus, 2009; Suzuki, 1989, 2002). Although it is true that, in the aggregate, AAPIs attend and graduate from higher education at a higher rate than other racial groups, several scholars have demonstrated the fact that AAPIs are not a homogeneous group and some Asian American subgroups suffer from drastic disparities in college access and success (Chang and others, 2007; Hune, 2002; Museus, 2009; Museus and Kiang, 2009; National Commission on Asian American and Pacific Islander Research in Education [CARE], 2008, 2010; Teranishi, 2007, 2010). In fact, researchers have shown that some ethnic groups within the Asian American category (e.g., Cambodian, Hmong, Laotian) and all ethnic groups within the Pacific Islander category (Native Hawaiian, Fijian, Guamanian, Marshallese, Samoan, Tongan) pursue higher education and attain a bachelor's degree at a rate lower than the national population (see Figure 5.1).

New Directions for Institutional Research, no. 151, Fall 2011 © Wiley Periodicals, Inc.
Published online in Wiley Online Library (wileyonlinelibrary.com) • DOI: 10.1002/ir.399

Figure 5.1. Bachelor's Degree Attainment Among Asian Americans by Ethnicity

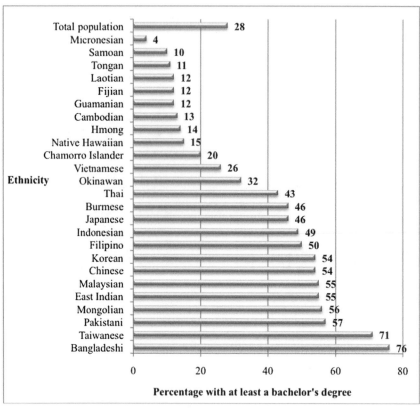

Data source: Public Use Microdata Sample (2007–2009).

Higher education researchers are increasingly recognizing that there is significant diversity within the AAPI population (CARE, 2008, 2010; Chang and others, 2007; Museus, 2009; Museus and Kiang, 2009; Teranishi, 2007, 2010), but most of the literature focuses on ethnic diversity. Consequently, higher education researchers, policymakers, and institutional leaders know relatively little about how other forms of diversity (socioeconomic, generational status, region of origin, etc.) shape college access and success among AAPIs. This lack of knowledge is problematic because it can lead to ill-informed and ineffective decision making among federal, state, and institutional policymakers and can even function to perpetuate barriers to and inequities in college access and success among AAPIs.

In this chapter, I discuss how researchers can use mixed-methods approaches and intersectional analyses to understand college access among first-generation AAPIs. First, I discuss the utility of mixed-methods approaches and intersectionality research in studying college access. Then, I discuss an introductory mixed-methods intersectional analysis of inequities in college access faced by first-generation AAPIs. I use the term *introductory mixed-methods* because I present the findings of a descriptive quantitative analysis and the initial themes that emerged from the analysis of qualitative interviews, recognizing that more complex quantitative and qualitative analyses could be conducted to extend this examination. Finally, I conclude with a set of recommendations for post-secondary education scholars and institutional researchers who consider using mixed methods and intersectionality in future research.

A couple of clarifications are worth mentioning before proceeding to the discussion. Whereas first-generation status can be conceptualized in many ways, for the purposes of this chapter I define *first-generation students* as those who do not have a parent with at least a bachelor's degree. In contrast, *continuing-generation students* are those students who have at least one parent with at least a bachelor's degree. And even though I understand the problematic nature of aggregating diverse AAPI ethnic groups into one category, I do so herein because the focus of this chapter is on the intersection between generational status and race, rather than ethnic diversity, differences, and disparities.

Utility of Intersectionality Research in Studying College Access Among Asian Americans and Pacific Islanders

Discussion of college access often revolves around comparison of categories of singular social groupings (for example, race, generational status, or socioeconomic status; Adelman, 1999, 2006; National Center for Education Statistics [NCES], 2010). It is, for example, common to see comparisons of AAPI, black, Latino, Native American, and white students' college enrollment rates. It is also common to see first-generation students' enrollment compared with that of their continuing-generation peers or low-income students' enrollment rate compared with those of their middle- and high-income counterparts. Such analyses, however, generate a limited understanding of disparities in college access. They often fail, for instance, to examine the nature and magnitude of the disparities in access to higher education faced by low-income or first-generation AAPIs.

Alternatively, as described in Chapter One of this volume, higher education researchers can use intersectional analyses—examinations that focus an analysis on intersecting social identities that mutually shape individual and group experiences—to shed light on disparities in college access faced by groups situated at these intersections (as with race and generational status). Because intersectionality research focuses on intersecting identities and social groupings, it inherently incorporates a heightened level of complexity into empirical analyses (see McCall, 2005, for discussion of this complexity). Therefore, intersectional analyses can help higher education researchers identify disparities within social groups, in addition to inequities across those groupings.

Utility of Mixed-Methods Approaches to Studying College Access Among Asian Americans and Pacific Islanders

Research on and knowledge of college access among AAPIs is sparse. Most of the research that does exist uses quantitative methods to study college access among AAPIs (see, for example, Hurtado, Inkelas, Briggs, and Rhee, 1997; Teranishi and others, 2004). Quantitative inquiries have proven useful for comparing AAPIs to other racial groups, and these analyses typically show that AAPIs have a higher level of access to higher education than other populations (Adelman, 1999, 2006; NCES, 2010). However, quantitative analyses can also be useful for examining disparities in college access within the AAPI population. Teranishi and colleagues (2004), for example, demonstrated that Chinese and Korean Americans are much more likely to attend highly selective institutions than their Filipino and Southeast Asian American counterparts. They also showed that Asian Americans from high-income families are much more likely than those from low-income backgrounds to attend highly selective institutions.

Though researchers have also examined college access and choice among AAPIs (Hurtado, Inkelas, Briggs, and Rhee, 1997; Teranishi and others, 2004), there is still little understanding of the factors that influence specific AAPIs' access to college. Qualitative methods are particularly useful for this purpose because they can generate an in-depth understanding of AAPI student perceptions regarding what aspects of their experience were most influential in hindering or promoting their pursuit of and enrollment in postsecondary education. Thus both quantitative and qualitative methods can be useful in understanding AAPI students' access to college.

Mixed-Method Intersectional Analysis of Inequities in College Access Faced by First-Generation Asian Americans and Pacific Islanders

In this section, I describe a mixed-methods analysis of first-generation AAPI students' access to college. The purpose of the analysis was to examine whether first-generation AAPI students suffer from inequities in college access and explore explanations for those inequities. Specifically, two main research questions laid a foundation for the analysis: Do first-generation AAPIs face inequities in college access? What factors explain the inequities in college access faced by first-generation AAPI students?

NEW DIRECTIONS FOR INSTITUTIONAL RESEARCH • DOI: 10.1002/ir

The current analysis falls under the category of intersectionality research because it is focused on understanding the experiences of a population that is situated at the intersections of multiple identities (AAPI and first-generation student identities). A mixed-method approach was employed for this analysis because the first research question was best answered using quantitative methods, while the second question was best informed by qualitative techniques. Thus the current inquiry offers an example of how mixed methods can be applied to understand college access issues of an often-ignored population effectively.

There are several important considerations in designing and conducting a mixed-methods inquiry (for a more thorough discussion of these considerations, see Chapter Two). Though it is not an exhaustive list, I describe some issues researchers must consider.

Emphasis. Emphasis has to do with whether the quantitative or qualitative components of the study will be equally (i.e., equivalent) or disproportionately (quantitative dominant or qualitative dominant) emphasized. For the purposes of this inquiry, both quantitative and qualitative methods played a critical role in answering a central research question. Therefore, this inquiry was based on an equivalent design.

Timing. Timing refers to whether the quantitative and qualitative components will be concurrent (occurring simultaneously) or sequential (occurring in sequence with one component following another). For the current analysis, national quantitative data were collected a priori and used to understand whether inequities exist in access to college for the AAPI population, and qualitative data were subsequently used to explain the factors that might contribute to those inequities to college access. Thus, a quantitative → qualitative sequential design was employed.

Purpose. Finally, it is important to define the purpose of the method mixing. For the current analysis, the intent was to use qualitative methods to help build on and explain the findings generated from the quantitative component of the inquiry.

After consideration of the aforementioned factors, a follow-up explanation design was selected to guide the current inquiry. In explanatory follow-up designs, quantitative data are collected and analyzed before qualitative data and analysis; quantitative data are emphasized, and qualitative data are used to help explain the findings generated by a quantitative analysis (Creswell and Plano Clark, 2007). Because qualitative individual interview data were used to expand on the results of an analysis of quantitative data from a national survey, an explanatory follow-up approach was deemed appropriate.

The Quantitative Analysis

The quantitative data in the current analysis were collected as part of a nationally representative longitudinal study conducted by the National

Center for Education Statistics, which is housed within the U.S. Department of Education. The Education Longitudinal Study (ELS: 02/06) administered a survey to a nationally representative sample of high school sophomores in 2002. Follow-up surveys were administered in 2004 and 2006. The ELS has collected information about students' high school experiences as well as data on college access. In addition, the ELS collected important background data (such as race, ethnicity, and parent's education level), which permits comparison of college access by those background characteristics. For the purposes of this analysis, the unweighted sample was limited to 1,460 AAPI students. Appropriate cross-sectional and panel weights were applied and the weighted sample sizes are displayed below the figures presented here.

The ELS data were analyzed using descriptive statistics and Pearson's chi-square tests. Specifically, I used descriptive statistics to examine whether generational status was related to several college-access-related factors among AAPIs, and Pearson's chi-square tests were used to determine whether those relationships were statistically significant. The chi-square results indicate that, compared to their continuing-generation counterparts, first-generation AAPIs exhibited significantly lower educational expectations, took college entrance examinations at a significantly lower rate, applied to and matriculated into colleges and universities at a significantly lower rate, and (among those who did matriculate) were significantly less likely to matriculate into a four-year institution (all statistically significant at the .001 level). Figures 5.2 through 5.5 display the descriptive statistics, including a visual depiction of the differences between first-generation and continuing-generation students.

Precollege Inequities. The path to college begins much earlier than the senior year of high school. Environments and experiences during K–12 education lead to formation of students' expectations regarding how far they will go in their education, which then has an impact on their progress through the education pipeline (Allen, 1992; Astin, 1977; Carter, 1999; Epps, 1995; Museus, Harper, and Nichols, 2010; Pascarella and Terenzini, 1991, 2005). As is shown in Figure 5.2, first-generation AAPI high school sophomores exhibit significantly lower expectations than their continuing-generation peers. Indeed, a lower percentage of first-generation (23 percent) than continuing-generation (39 percent) AAPI students expect to attain a Ph.D. or professional degree. In addition, over twice as many first-generation AAPI high school sophomores expect to attain less than a bachelor's degree as do their continuing-generation peers (10 and 4 percent, respectively).

For students to attend most institutions of higher education, they must take a college entrance examination (ACT or SAT). Thus, whether students have taken such exams could be an important predictor of matriculating into an institution of higher education. As Figure 5.3 shows, first-generation AAPI students (71 percent) are much less likely than their

Figure 5.2. Educational Expectations Among Asian American and Pacific Islander High School Sophomores by Generational Status in 2002

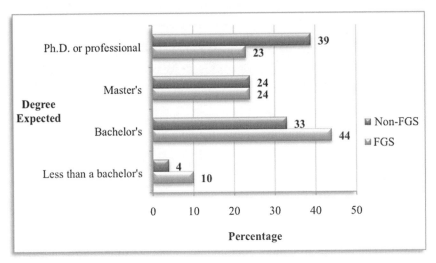

Note: Weighted N = 142,517.

Figure 5.3. Entrance Examination Activity Among Asian American Pacific Islander High School Seniors by Generational Status

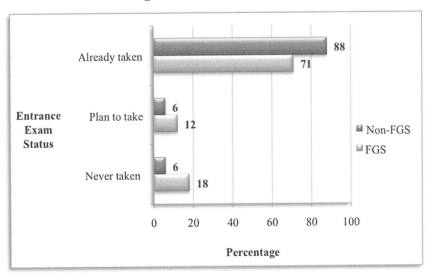

Note: Weighted N = 122,228.

Figure 5.4. College Application and Matriculation Activity Among Asian American and Pacific Islanders by Generational Status

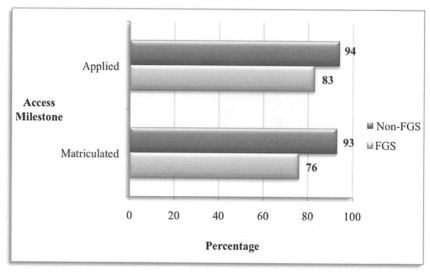

Note: Weighted N = 121,029 (applied) and 121,137 (matriculated).

Figure 5.5. Level of First Postsecondary Institution Among Asian American and Pacific Islanders by Generational Status

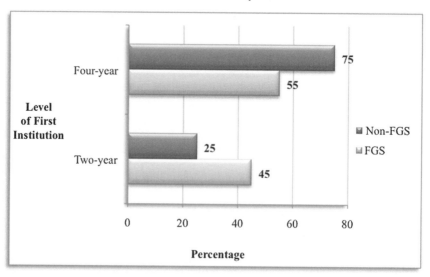

Note: Weighted N = 100,336.

continuing-generation peers (88 percent) to have taken a college entrance examination by the spring of their senior year in high school.

College Application and Entrance Inequities. Disparities between first-generation and continuing-generation AAPIs also exist in whether they apply to a postsecondary institution, whether they matriculate at a college or university, and the type of institution they enter. As shown in Figure 5.4, significantly fewer first-generation than continuing-generation AAPIs apply to (83 to 94 percent, respectively) and matriculate into (76 to 93 percent, respectively) institutions of higher education. Finally, among AAPIs who matriculate at a two- or four-year institution, first-generation AAPIs (55 percent) are much less likely than their continuing-generation peers (75 percent) to enter a four-year college or university (see Figure 5.5).

The Qualitative Analysis

The quantitative analysis demonstrated that first-generation AAPIs appear to face inequities in college access, which manifest in lower educational expectations as well as decreased likelihood of taking college entrance examinations, applying to institutions of higher education, matriculating into a college or university, and enrolling in a four-year university. However, the quantitative analysis was limited in explaining the causes of those inequities. To address this limitation, qualitative data were collected through interviews with thirty first-generation AAPI undergraduates who identified with eight ethnic groups and were enrolled at six four-year institutions to generate a more in-depth understanding of the inequities in access faced by first-generation AAPIs. The thirty participants were purposefully selected based on three criteria: they (1) self-identified as Asian American or Pacific Islander, (2) indicated that neither of their parents earned a four-year college degree, and (3) were enrolled in a two- or four-year degree-granting postsecondary institution.

Sixty- to ninety-minute in-person interviews were conducted with all participants. During the interviews, participants were asked about factors that hindered or contributed to their pursuit of a college education. Those interviews were professionally transcribed, the data were subsequently organized in the NVivo Qualitative Software Research Package, and open- and axial-coding procedures were used to identify emergent themes and the properties of those themes (Strauss and Corbin, 1998). Whereas open coding refers to the process of identifying, labeling, categorizing, and describing phenomena found in the interview transcripts, axial coding is focused on identifying relationships among codes. Four themes emerged as salient challenges to students' pursuit of a college education.

Anti-College Cultures. A majority of interview participants originated from low-income neighborhoods and schools. Some of them reported living in neighborhood communities and attending high schools in which it was not normal for students to pursue higher education, and they were discouraged from seeking a college degree by peers, teachers, or counselors.

Financial Constraints. Participants discussed how financial constraints influenced their decisions about whether to pursue higher education and where to apply. Finances influenced students by causing them to question whether they should attend college, influencing them to choose a college close to home, and giving them reason to attend a less-expensive institution.

Alone in the Application and Choice Processes. Participants' parents never went through the process of applying to and choosing a college, so they could not help those students navigate these processes. The inability of parents to guide students through these processes and the fact that a majority of participants found teachers and counselors to be only marginally helpful led to participants' feeling they had to navigate the process alone.

Excess Pressure. The single most salient positive influence on participants' decisions to pursue higher education was the high expectations held by their parents. They noted that, from a young age, they were expected to go to college; the participants also highlighted the importance of those expectations in shaping their attitudes about higher education. They underscored the positive impact of their parents' support on their going to college. In a few cases, however, the pressure became excessive or was not accompanied by support, which led to a few students becoming discouraged.

Extensions of the Preceding Introductory Analyses

The preceding sections provide a preliminary understanding of generational differences in college access-related outcomes and the factors that students perceive to influence their college-going behavior among AAPI students, but much remains to be learned about college access among first-generation and continuing-generation AAPIs. For example, researchers can extend the quantitative analysis herein by examining differences in the effects of various predictors on college access across generational status; in fact, such analysis is already under way. Researchers could also quantify the factors that emerged from our qualitative findings and examine whether they are statistically associated with access among first-generation and continuing-generation students. In addition, future research could extend the qualitative findings here by conducted qualitative analyses of the factors that influence college access that disaggregate by generational status. Such disaggregation would allow researchers to understand more thoroughly how various phenomena influence access among first-generation and continuing-generation AAPIs and how the nature of those relationships varies across those two subgroups.

Lessons Learned from the Mixed-Method Intersectional Analysis

Few would argue with the notion that higher education research is problem-based. For scholars and institutional researchers to deem an inquiry worthy of their time, they must identify a problem and design a study that can help generate solutions to that problem (Creswell, 2003; Maxwell, 2004; Museus and Chang, 2009). In the preceding example, the quantitative analysis offered clarification that a problem exists by highlighting the inequities in college access faced by first-generation AAPI students. Complementarily, the qualitative analysis offered more in-depth understanding of the factors that might contribute to the problem of inequities in college access faced by first-generation AAPIs, which can lead to knowledge regarding how to address the sources of those inequalities. For example, the qualitative theme of first-generation AAPI students navigating anti-college cultures highlights the importance of educational policymakers and leaders advocating for college-going subcultures (for example, community organizations with education services and college preparation programs) that can help foster college-going philosophies among those students. Thus it is the combination of quantitative and qualitative approaches that generated a holistic picture that can help K–12 and higher education scholars, educational policymakers, institutional researchers, and institutional leaders understand the educational problem and how it might be addressed.

Think Critically About Categories in Comparative Analyses. Analyses that rely only on racial categorizations, or any single type of social classifications for that matter, can be misleading (see Chapter One for in-depth discussion). Researchers should think critically about such examinations and consider the realities that are masked by overreliance on analyses that compare racial or socioeconomic groups. In the preceding analysis, focusing on a group that is situated at the intersection of race and generational status led to an understanding of the inequities faced by this group, as well as the mechanisms by which those inequities emerged and are perpetuated. Thus such a focus on groups that are situated at the intersections can lead to higher education scholars and institutional researchers developing a more holistic and accurate understanding of students in postsecondary education.

Consider Characteristics of Design Before Selecting One. Because there are so many ways to combine quantitative and qualitative data, no typology is likely to encompass all types of mixed-methods approaches (Creswell and Plano Clark, 2007), and researchers might find it difficult to classify an inquiry as a specific type of mixed-methods research design. Researchers should ask several questions prior to selecting a mixed-methods design to guide their investigation, about emphasis, timing, mixing, and purpose. These decisions can help clarify what type of mixed-methods approach is ideal for a given investigation. Once the answers to these questions are clarified, researchers can more easily designate the ideal mixed-methods approach to their inquiry.

Consider the Range of Potential Data Combinations. Some mixed-methods research designs consist of researchers both collecting and analyzing quantitative and qualitative data, but not all mixed-methods inquiries necessarily fall into this category. For the preceding mixed-methods analysis, quantitative data were collected a priori (beforehand) by the U.S. Department of Education, rather than by the researcher. Combining these precollected national survey data and the qualitative interview data, however, was most effective in understanding whether the population being examined faced inequities in college access and understanding what factors might explain those disparities. Researchers should therefore consider the wide range of potential combinations between using existing data and collecting original empirical data to answer their research questions most effectively.

References

Adelman, C. *Answers in the Toolbox: Academic Intensity, Attendance Patterns, and Bachelor's Degree Attainment.* Washington, D.C.: U.S. Department of Education, 1999.

Adelman, C. *The Toolbox Revisited: Paths to Degree Completion from High School Through College.* Washington, D.C.: U.S. Department of Education, 2006.

Allen, W. R. "The Color of Success: African-American College Student Outcomes at Predominantly White and Historically Black Public Colleges and Universities." *Harvard Education Review*, 1992, 62(1), 26–44.

Astin, A. *Four Critical Years.* San Francisco: Jossey-Bass, 1977.

Carter, D. F. "The Impact of Institutional Choice and Environments on African American and White Students' Degree Expectations." *Research in Higher Education*, 1999, 40(1), 17–41.

Chang, M. J., Park, J. J., Lin, M. H., Poon, O. A., and Nakanishi, D. T. *Beyond Myths: The Growth and Diversity of Asian American College Freshmen, 1971–2005.* Los Angeles: Higher Education Research Institute, 2007.

Creswell, J. W. *Research Design: Qualitative, Quantitative, and Mixed-Methods Approaches* (2nd ed.). Thousand Oaks, Calif.: Sage, 2003.

Creswell, J. W., and Plano Clark, V. L. *Designing and Conducting Mixed-Methods Research.* Thousand Oaks, Calif.: Sage, 2007.

Epps, E. G. "Race, Class, and Educational Opportunity: Trends in the Sociology of Education." *Sociological Forum*, 1995, 10(4), 593–608.

Hune, S. "Demographics and Diversity of Asian American College Students." In M. K. McEwen and others (eds.), *Working with Asian American College Students.* New Directions for Student Services, no. 97. San Francisco: Jossey-Bass, 2002.

Hurtado, S., Inkelas, K. K., Briggs, C., and Rhee, B. S. "Differences in College Access and Choice Among Racial Groups: Identifying Continuing Barriers." *Research in Higher Education*, 1997, 38(1), 43–75.

Maxwell, J. A. *Qualitative Research Design: An Integrative Approach* (2nd ed.). Thousand Oaks, Calif.: Sage, 2004.

McCall, L. "The Complexity of Intersectionality." *Journal of Women in Culture and Society*, 2005, 30(3), 1771–1800.

Museus, S. D. "A Critical Analysis of the Exclusion of Asian American from Higher Education Research and Discourse." In L. Zhan (ed.), *Asian American Voices: Engaging, Empowering, Enabling* (pp. 59–76). New York: NLN Press, 2009.

Museus, S. D., and Chang, M. J. "Rising to the Challenge of Conducting Research on Asian Americans in Higher Education." In S. D. Museus (ed.), *Conducting Research on Asian Americans in Higher Education.* New Directions for Institutional Research, no. 142. San Francisco: Jossey-Bass, 2009.

Museus, S. D., Harper, S. R., and Nichols, A. H. "Racial Differences in the Formation of Postsecondary Educational Expectations: A Structural Model." *Teachers College Record,* 2010, *112*(3). 811–842.

Museus, S. D., and Kiang, P. N. "The Model Minority Myth and How It Contributes to the Invisible Minority Reality in Higher Education Research." In S. D. Museus (ed.), *Conducting Research on Asian Americans in Higher Education.* New Directions for Institutional Research, no. 142. San Francisco: Jossey-Bass, 2009.

National Center for Education Statistics [NCES]. *The Condition of Education 2010.* Washington, D.C.: NCES, 2010.

National Commission on Asian American and Pacific Islander Research in Education [CARE]. *Facts, Not Fiction: Setting the Records Straight.* New York: CARE, 2008.

National Commission on Asian American and Pacific Islander Research in Education [CARE]. *Federal Higher Education Policy Priorities and the Asian American and Pacific Islander Community.* New York: CARE, 2010.

Pascarella, E. T., and Terenzini, P. T. *How College Affects Students.* San Francisco: Jossey-Bass, 1991.

Pascarella, E. T., and Terenzini, P. T. *How College Affects Students.* Vol. 2: *A Third Decade of Research.* San Francisco: Jossey-Bass, 2005.

Strauss, A., and Corbin, J. *Basics of Qualitative Research: Techniques and Procedures for Developing Grounded Theory.* Thousand Oaks, Calif.: Sage, 1998.

Suzuki, B. "Asian Americans as the 'Model Minority': Outdoing Whites? Or Media Hype?" *Change,* Nov.–Dec. 1989, 13–19.

Suzuki, B. "Revisiting the Model Minority Stereotype: Implications for Student Affairs Practice and Higher Education." In M. K. McEwen and others (eds.), *Working with Asian American College Students.* New Directions for Student Services, no. 97. San Francisco: Jossey-Bass, 2002.

Teranishi, R. T. "Race, Ethnicity, and Higher Education Policy: The Use of Critical Quantitative Research." In F. Stage (ed.), *Using Quantitative Research to Answer Critical Questions.* New Directions for Institutional Research, no 133. San Francisco: Jossey-Bass, 2007.

Teranishi, R. T. *Asians in the Ivory Tower: Dilemmas of Racial Inequality in American Higher Education.* New York: Teachers College Press, 2010.

Teranishi, R. T., Ceja, M., Antonio, A. L., Allen, W. R., and McDonough, P. "The College-Choice Process for Asian Pacific Americans: Ethnicity and Socioeconomic Class in Context." *Review of Higher Education,* 2004, *27*(4), 527–551.

SAMUEL D. MUSEUS is an assistant professor of educational administration at the University of Hawai'i Manoa.

6

This chapter uses a mixed-method approach to critically examine white male college students' racial ideologies and the experiences that influence racial ideology formation. It highlights both how racial privilege is recreated in higher education and how mixed-methods and intersectionality approaches to institutional research allow more robust analytical possibilities.

Using a Sequential Exploratory Mixed-Method Design to Examine Racial Hyperprivilege in Higher Education

Nolan L. Cabrera

After President Obama's 2010 State of the Union address, MSNBC commentator Chris Matthews offered this reaction, "It's interesting: [President Obama] is postracial, by all appearances. I forgot he was black tonight for an hour." Immediately after the election of a person of color to the presidency, the idea of being "postracial" seeped into the national media, essentially claiming that racism was over. David Horowitz (2009) provided his own version of this sentiment, stating that for someone to argue that racism persists "is impossible to square with the fact that we have an African American president who was elected by mainly non-African American voters."

Despite this popular rhetoric, the United States is far from a "postracial" society (Bonilla-Silva and Ray, 2009). Systemic racism continues to inequitably stratify society in favor of white people at the expense of people of color (Feagin, 2006; Omi and Winant, 1994), and this system of racial inequality is called white supremacy (Bonilla-Silva, 2006). Institutions of higher education within a white supremacist structure are not simply neutral arbiters; rather they serve as means of both reinforcing and sometimes challenging systemic racism (Cabrera, 2009). Racial ideologies are a central component of racial stratification (Bonilla-Silva, 2006); however, both higher education and institutional researchers have spent little time examining how college affects students' racial ideology development. In this chapter, I describe an intersectionality, sequential exploratory, mixed-methods inquiry into racial ideology formation of white male

New Directions for Institutional Research, no. 151, Fall 2011 © Wiley Periodicals, Inc.
Published online in Wiley Online Library (wileyonlinelibrary.com) • DOI: 10.1002/ir.400

undergraduates. I also discuss the implications of this inquiry for institutional researchers.

Intersectionality

Intersectionality research is both dynamic and underused in higher education and institutional research. Intersectionality pushes beyond reliance on singular social groupings (e.g., races *or* genders) to richer, more informative analyses that can concurrently account for multiple systems of oppression (Hancock, 2007a). In particular, intersectionality challenges identity politics, where group solidarity, and sometimes group essentialism, is assumed as a foundational component of a social movement (Hancock, 2007b). As Kimberlé Crenshaw (1994) argues, "feminist efforts to politicize experiences of women and antiracist efforts to politicize experiences of people of color have frequently proceeded as though the issues and experiences they each detail occur on mutually exclusive terrains" (p. 94). Focusing on intersectionality complicates such isolated conceptualizations of gender or racial oppression.

From its inception, intersectionality research has focused on critical examination of multiple social identities as they are contextualized within systems of oppression. Within higher education literature, there is a dearth of intersectionality research, which is not surprising since there is little empirical research on intersectionality in general (Hancock, 2007a). There is some research emerging regarding underrepresentation of men of color in higher education (e.g., College Board, 2010; Riegle-Crumb, 2010; Sáenz and Ponjuan, 2009), but this work fails to take account of the power structures that continue to favor men in society, and it tends to be primarily analyses of difference as opposed to illuminating hierarchical relationships. Institutional leaders and researchers may replicate these patterns as they conduct self-studies of their own campuses. Analyses focusing on the experiences of women in STEM or perceptions of climate among lesbian, bisexual, gay, and transgendered (LGBT) students are frequently decontextualized from larger social structures of privilege and marginalization.

Further, when intersectional analyses are conducted, virtually all studies focus on the disadvantaged. Rarely, if at all, does intersectionality research interrogate systemic privilege. This makes sense as intersectionality research was originally meant to carve out safe physical, emotional, and intellectual spaces for marginalized communities. However, there is a dialectical relationship between oppressed and oppressor: there cannot be one without the other. Thus, interrogating racial privilege can be a complimentary effort to empowering antiracist movements. Within this context, an interrogation of whiteness becomes warranted, but is whiteness formation uniform across genders? If white men experience white privilege that is compounded by male privilege (i.e., racial hyperprivilege), could this racial hyperprivilege affect formation of their racial ideology?

NEW DIRECTIONS FOR INSTITUTIONAL RESEARCH • DOI: 10.1002/ir

Racial Ideology

The undergraduate years tend to be a time of great cognitive and social development (Evans and others, 2010), which is an area often given a great deal of attention by institutional researchers who aim to learn more about student growth on campus. However, student racial ideology development is virtually unexplored and rarely the subject of research. Like intersectionality, ideology is a term that differs substantially between its colloquial and academic usages. It is commonly used as a synonym for political affiliation, but scholars of racism identify racial ideology as integral to perpetuation of racial inequality. As Bonilla-Silva (2006) argues, "the central components of any dominant racial ideology is [sic] it frames or *sets pathways for interpreting information*" (p. 26, emphasis in original).

Bonilla-Silva (2006) argues that racial ideologies represent more than an individual preference (that is, racial attitudes), and they reveal a collective racial group interest. Within this context, racial ideologies serve as the dominant group's method of justifying their social dominance. Bonilla-Silva (2006) suggests that the dominant racial ideology is one of *color-blind racism*, and it consists of four central frames. First, abstract liberalism is support for equality but opposition to race-conscious policies. Second, naturalization describes segregation as a function of individual choice. Third, cultural racism is inequality as a defect in the culture of racial minorities. Finally, minimization of racism is a belief that racism is no longer a pertinent social issue. Bonilla-Silva and Forman (2000) argue that the dominant college student racial ideology is color-blind racism, but their findings do not demonstrate the role that campus environment plays in the development of these ideologies.

Racial and other ideologies can be either hierarchy-enhancing or hierarchy-attenuating, depending on whether a person's worldview is more in support of inequality (hierarchy-enhancing) or egalitarianism (hierarchy-attenuating; Sidanius and Pratto, 1999). In their work on social dominance orientation, Sidanius and Pratto (1999) demonstrate that those who are in the most privileged social locations (e.g., men, wealthy people, and white people) tend to subscribe to hierarchy-enhancing ideologies, while those who have socially marginalized identities (e.g., women, poor, and nonwhite people) tend to subscribe to hierarchy-attenuating ideologies. Intersectionality and racial ideology provide the context for the mixed-methods inquiry into the impact of campus environments on white male racial ideology described in this chapter.

An Exploratory Mixed-Methods Inquiry into Campus Environments and White Male Racial Ideology

Hancock (2007b) argues that mixed methods are necessary to truly account for both the individual experiences and the systemic realities that continually recreate social stratification along multiple loci of oppression. Within this context, I discuss a mixed-methods approach to the study of the impact of college environments on white male college students' development of racial ideologies. Specifically, this study was conducted through implementation of a sequential exploratory mixed-methods approach, where the qualitative component precedes the quantitative element (Tashakkori and Teddlie, 2003). This design is ideal for explorations of new phenomena. As there is little empirical understanding of dominant racial ideology, the sequential exploratory mixed-methods approach serves as the ideal design for this inquiry. Here is a step-by-step overview of this process, and the findings resulting from each phase of analysis.

Step 1: Qualitative Instrumentation. I began with Bonilla-Silva's Detroit Area Study interview protocol (2006) as a starting point for investigating white male college student racial ideologies. This protocol included questions about definitions of racism, examples of racism, participants' support for or aversion to race-conscious social policies, and explanations for the persistence of racial inequality. The number of questions was reduced substantially, and they were reframed to focus more directly on issues of race within the college environment. For example, questions asked participants to spend time describing the racial diversity of their collegiate friendship groups, rather than the diversity of their neighborhoods.

Step 2: Site Selection. I selected two large, research, public institutions to serve as sites for the qualitative component of this inquiry: Western University (WU) and Southwestern University (SWU), both pseudonyms. I sought to understand whether institutional structures influenced the formation of racial ideologies. Therefore, I purposefully selected institutions that differ in compositional diversity. SWU is a predominantly white university, while racial minorities make up the majority of students attending WU. They also differ in selectivity, with WU admitting approximately 20 percent of its applicants, while SWU admits more than 80 percent. Finally, SWU practices affirmative action, while WU does not.

Step 3: Participant Recruitment. Because racial ideology and political ideology are highly correlated (Sidanius and Pratto, 1999), I purposefully recruited students from a diversity of political orientations to hear a wide range of voices. Recruiting the participants was difficult for two reasons. First, students tended not to respond to email requests to participate in the interviews. Second, I had no funding to offer an incentive for participation. To address these two issues, I used the WU and SWU websites to find student organizations with either an explicit or implicit political orientation (e.g., campus Democrats, campus Republicans, fraternities, Objectivists, and Students for a Democratic Society). I sent email requests to the leadership of approximately fifteen student organizations at each institution, requesting thirty seconds to recruit in person at their weekly meetings. The recruitment strategy yielded twenty-eight participants (WU, $n = 15$; SWU, $n = 13$) across the two institutions from a range of political orientations.

Step 4: Interview Procedures. Participants were interviewed in a location of their preference. If they had no preference, interviews were held in offices around campus. I racially self-identified as Chicano, which is my primary racial identity, at the beginning of each interview so that my racial ambiguity did not differentially influence the dialogue. At the end of the interviews, I asked how much participants thought about my racial background during these discussions of race. Almost uniformly, they said they did not. Part of this was a function of my light skin, use of "standard English," and ability to "pass" as white. Interviews lasted approximately forty-five minutes. The interviews were transcribed verbatim and thematically coded using a pattern-matching technique (Yin, 1994) to identify emergent themes in relation to existent literature on racial ideologies.

Step 5: Qualitative Analysis. I analyzed the transcripts of participants' narratives and found four dominant racial ideology frames. These themes suggest participants subscribed to a slightly modified version of Bonilla-Silva's *color-blind racism* ideology. Their four frames were (1) whiteness as normal, (2) racism of minimal importance, (3) the United States as meritocratic, and (4) opposition to race-conscious social policies.

Whiteness as Normal. Participants tended to come from either racially homogeneous neighborhoods or ones where they were consistently in the majority. Of the twenty-eight participants, only five lived in neighborhoods where whites were not the majority; five attended high schools where whites were not the majority. These numbers do not tell the full story because, as Brandon (WU) conveyed, "An interesting thing was AP [advanced placement] classes. Like, there was maybe like one or two black and Latino or Chicano person in those classes . . . and the rest was mostly Asian and whatever white kids were left." Thus high school internal segregation further exacerbated the separation of the races.

Trevor (WU) also asserted that few precollege cross-racial interactions existed, and for very specific purposes. He elaborated, "There were a very few, small number of black people in my school. No one interacted with them except to buy drugs." In Trevor's experience, not only did he have a physical separation from his black peers but also interactions, when they did occur, were primarily functional in nature (as in white students wanting drugs). When asked to report the race of their three best friends in college, 86 percent of participants reported the majority of their friends were white. Again, their "normal" racial experience meant being in the majority. As Duncan (SWU) explained, "People tend to like the company of others that share similar values, similar, I guess, life experiences as them, and it just so happens that people in your same ethnic group or racial category have similar values."

NEW DIRECTIONS FOR INSTITUTIONAL RESEARCH • DOI: 10.1002/ir

Racism Is of Minimal Importance. Most participants defined racism as some type of overt hatred or inner disdain of racial minorities, which was framed as either a relic of the past or contained within fringe groups. For example, Ryan (WU) offered this: "It's hard because we live in California and California's such a diverse state that, I mean, I'm sure there's people here that could be similar, you know, associate with the KKK. But I mean, in my experience, I've never met anyone."

Martin (SWU) also believed that racism exists but is contained within groups outside his lived experience: "There's plenty of things that white people do that I don't like, like certain groups of people . . . Nazi skinheads, right, OK?" By claiming that he does not like Nazi skinheads, he was able to both condemn racism and frame himself as nonracist.

Some participants expressed a view that racism was a relic of the past, and therefore they bear no responsibility. As Dwight (SWU) explained, "I mean, I had no part in owning slaves, so I've never been that person to be prejudiced towards anybody because of that." Dwight then used this as a way to frame his opposition to affirmative action. According to him, because he feels no ill will toward racial minorities and had no part in owning slaves, he should not be "penalized" via race-conscious programs. The privileges of his whiteness remained invisible to him as he rhetorically practiced what Pierce (2003) refers to as "racing for innocence," where he acknowledges racial inequality exists but has no personal responsibility in creating a solution. Jonathan (WU) articulated a similar sentiment: "But it's almost like [racial minorities] try to pin [racism] on people nowadays, you know, the faults of people in the past."

The United States as Meritocratic. Most participants agreed that racial inequality exists, but relied on articulations of the American Dream as their solution to racial inequality. They tended to argue that, if racial minorities want to succeed, they have ample opportunity to do so if they are willing to work hard (meaning, racism is not a structural barrier for racial minorities). Martin (SWU) critiqued a "welfare culture" that he argued is endemic within minority communities:

There's a welfare culture among some black people for example. Not all black people. It exists among some Hispanic people. The idea that you don't . . . lack of accountability for your actions, lack of responsibility, the idea that you don't really have to work very hard to succeed.

Within Martin's understanding, racial inequality is a function of liberal social policies that undercut the minority work ethic. To him, the problem is a lack of responsibility that leads to laziness, and racism is not the issue as he framed the United States to be generally open and meritocratic.

Others viewed work ethic as the pathway toward upward mobility. Andy (WU) succinctly argued, "If people work hard, they will succeed. I believe that. That's what I believe." For Andy, there was no need for further examination or explanation. He took it as an article of faith that hard work leads to success, and that was as far as he was willing to explore the issue. Derek (WU) was more direct in asserting that the system is open to all willing to work hard, and racism has nothing to do with structuring opportunity:

> I think it's because I personally don't . . . like race is not really an issue in the sense that it's like it doesn't matter what race you are, you can attain anything, you can do whatever you want, you can marry whoever you want.

Many would think that Derek already achieved a great deal in his life by attending an academically selective institution of higher education. Therefore, for him, it was almost a matter of common sense to believe that the American system is truly open and meritocratic to those willing to work.

Opposition to Race-Conscious Social Policies. Finally, the participants tended to strongly oppose race-conscious social policies, which they framed as either racist or, at the least, unfair to white people. For example, Ryan (WU) described his beliefs about affirmative action: "If a company needs to fill a quota, then they'll hire the black guy. And that's not fair. . . . The white guy who worked harder and uh, had a better education, or studied more, or whatever it was that his situation is, just because he's white, he doesn't get the job, or he doesn't get to go to the school he wants to."

Ryan was one of many participants who described affirmative action as a quota system, even though quotas were outlawed in the *Regents of the University of California v. Bakke* (1978) decision about thirty years before this research occurred.

The sources of this information tended to come from personal observations that the participants made regarding diversity on their campus or in the workplace. Hoyt (WU) was absolutely opposed to affirmative action because "it's fighting racism with more racism." However, the experiences that led him to this understanding were telling:

> A: That is primarily an opinion of mine derived from observation where I see different . . . businesses, primarily small businesses, or franchises that have probably a majority staff of minority workers.
>
> Q: Could you give me an example?
>
> A: There is a local Burger King, which appears to be primarily staffed by Latinos. I haven't yet seen, to my knowledge, one white person there. But there may be somewhere I can't see.

There is a certain absurdity to Hoyt seeing affirmative action limiting his life chances as evidenced by the racially homogeneous Burger King environment. However, he did truly feel marginalized by affirmative action, even if these feelings did not represent a tangible reality.

Step 6: Framing the Quantitative Analysis. The narratives of the twenty-eight participants created the exploratory component of the sequential exploratory mixed-methods design. The quantitative analysis of this research was undertaken for two reasons: to (1) examine whether the four frames of participants' racial ideologies are generalizable to a larger population, and (2) explore the role that the college environment plays in shaping racial ideologies. I conducted the quantitative analysis at a single institutional site, SWU.

While the qualitative component of the research was completed, a longitudinal survey research project on undergraduates at SWU was constructed and conducted by a research group of which I was a part. A large number of the constructs on the survey addressed experiences with racism and views on social issues related to race. I was able to identify three of the four central racial ideology frames in the survey constructs, and the fourth (whiteness as normal) had some proxies that were sufficiently similar.

The survey was administered to students at SWU before their freshman year and again during the middle of the second semester of the first year. The survey captured constructs related to experiences in the campus environment (such as involvement in campus groups), as well as goals, aspirations, self-assessments, and views on social issues. In alignment with pretest-posttest survey designs, all racial ideology questions were asked in both waves of the survey. The first wave was administered to participants before they began classes ($n = 1,400$ out of 6,966 incoming freshmen). The second wave was administered in the middle of spring semester. Forty-three percent of the students in the first wave responded to the second survey ($n = 593$). All of the dimensions of students' racial ideologies were asked in both surveys. Of these 593 participants who completed both surveys, 104 were self-identified white men.

Step 7: Factor Analysis. Once variables that matched the qualitatively identified racial ideology were identified, I conducted confirmatory factor analyses to determine whether racial ideology factor structures were consistent across a larger population. I also wanted to ensure the racial ideology construct was consistent during both survey administrations. Table 6.1 displays the survey questions that composed the racial ideology construct.

The first four components fall within the tenet of opposition to race-conscious policies, the fifth and sixth components represent America as meritocratic, the next frames whiteness as normal, and the final two fall within the frame of racism being of minimal importance. For both the total sample of entering students and the overall sample of students after their first year of college, the factor held together well, with Cronbach's alphas of .769 and .818, respectively. After I determined the reliability of the racial ideology construct, I also ran separate confirmatory factor

Table 6.1. Racial Ideology Factors, Components, and Measurements

	Time 1 (n = 593); α = .769	Time 2 (n = 593); α = .818
Incorporating writings and research about different ethnic groups and women into courses (reverse-coded)[1]	.562	.631
Establishing center for students from different racial groups (reverse-coded)[1]	.579	.650
Hiring more faculty of color should be a top priority of this university (reverse-coded)[2]	.690	.770
Colleges should aggressively recruit more students of color (reverse-coded)[2]	.709	.784
The system prevents people of color from getting their fair share of good jobs and better pay (reverse-coded)[2]	.692	.723
Many whites lack an understanding of the problems that people from different racial/ethnic groups face (reverse-coded)[2]	.543	.612
Our society has done enough to promote the welfare of different racial/ethnic groups[2]	.628	.551
Racial discrimination is no longer a problem in the US[2]	.509	.525

[1] Scale: 1 = strongly oppose; 4 = strongly support
[2] Scale: 1 = strongly disagree; 4 = strongly agree

analyses for white men, white women, nonwhite men, and nonwhite women to see if it held across these four groups. The racial ideology construct held together across these groups and across both samples; all Cronbach's alphas were higher than 0.700.

Step 8: ANOVA and Scheffe's Test. Once I determined that the racial ideology construct held together as a factor, I wanted to test if white male undergraduates had more hierarchy-enhancing or hierarchy-attenuating racial ideologies than their nonwhite and female peers. To do this, I created four categories of students: white men, white women, nonwhite men, and nonwhite women. Then I ran an analysis of variance (ANOVA) to see if there were significant differences among these four groups in terms of their racial ideologies (see Table 6.2).

The ANOVA confirmed that significant differences existed at both survey administration time points, but it did not permit determination of which groups differed in terms of their racial ideologies (significant at the .001 level). To address this issue, I employed a Scheffe's post hoc test. As I was primarily interested in examining white male racial ideologies, I will present the Scheffe results only in relation to the white male students.

Consistent with Sidanius and Pratto (1999), the most systemically privileged students surveyed in this study (white men) had the most hierarchy-enhancing racial ideologies of the four groups (see Table 6.3).

Table 6.2. ANOVA Results for Racial Ideology

		Sum of Squares	Df	Mean Square	F	Sig.
Racial ideology, Time 1	Between groups	52.58	3	17.53	21.51	.000***
	Within groups	479.88	589	.82		
	Total	532.46	592			
Racial ideology, Time 2	Between groups	60.12	3	20.04	25.97	.000***
	Within groups	454.52	589	.77		
	Total	514.64	592			

Note: * p <0.05, ** p <0.01, *** p <0.001.

Table 6.3. Scheffe Post Hoc Test, White Male Racial Ideology vs. Women and People of Color

			Mean Difference	Standard Error	Sig.
Racial ideology, Time 1	White men	Nonwhite women	.85	.11	.000***
	White men	Nonwhite men	.58	.14	.001**
	White men	White women	.32	.10	.027
Racial ideology, Time 2	White men	Nonwhite women	.87	.11	.000***
	White men	Nonwhite men	.57	.13	.001**
	White men	White women	.25	.10	.110

Note: * p <0.05, ** p <0.01, *** p <0.001.

Specifically, white men had significantly more hierarchy-enhancing racial ideologies than the other three groups at both time points, with the exception of white women during the second survey.

Conversely, the most systemically marginalized students (women of color) had the most hierarchy-attenuating racial ideologies. During the initial survey, there were significant differences between white male racial ideologies and the other three groups, but the differences between white men and white women were significant only at the 0.05 level. The second survey produced similar results. The differences between white men and people of color, regardless of gender, remained significant at the .01 or .001 level, but the difference between white men and white women became nonsignificant ($p = 0.110$).

Step 9: Ordinary Least Squares Regression Analysis. The purpose of this research was not only to identify the central frames of racial ideology but also understand the college experiences that affect their formation. Therefore, the final component of the quantitative analysis involved running two separate ordinary least squares (OLS) regression models: one of exclusively white men and the other of people of color and women. The regression models tested the first-year college experiences that, after controlling for incoming student racial ideology, affected those students' racial ideologies in their first year of college. I was limited in the number of independent variables I could select because of the relatively small number of white men completing both surveys. Moreover, I wanted to see how the college environment affected racial ideology development, so I primarily focused independent variables on college experiences (see Table 6.4). The modeling used the enter method of variable selection.

As there was little change in white male student racial ideologies, it was not surprising that, after controlling for precollege racial ideologies, there was only one measure significantly related to ideology change (see Table 6.4). Specifically, the frequency of discussions on race significantly predicted a more hierarchy-attenuating racial ideology ($\beta = -.18*$). Other diversity-related activities such as in-class discussions of race/ethnicity

Table 6.4. Predictors of First-Year Racial Ideology

	White Men (n = 104)		Nonwhite Men (n = 489)	
	r	β	r	β
Racial ideology, Time 1	.72***	.70***	.65***	.56***
Number of classes taken that had materials or readings on race/ethnicity issues[1]	−.27**	−.08	−.24***	−.14***
Frequency: engaged in discussions about racial/ethnic issues in class[2]	−.26**	−.05	−.12**	.07
Frequency: discussed racial/ethnic issues[2]	−.30**	−.18*	−.26***	−.10*
Frequency: cross-racial interactions[2]	−.05	.16	−.08*	−.00
Frequency: ethnic center participation[2]	−.14	−.06	−.28***	−.05
Frequency: participation in an organization promoting cultural diversity[2]	−.13	.02	−.21***	−.02
Frequency: interactions with Caucasians/ whites[3]	−.09	.00	.22***	.07*
Racial/ethnic composition of friendship groups[4]	.11	.11	.32***	.08*
	Adjusted $R^2 = .58$		Adjusted $R^2 = .47$	

Notes: * p <0.05, ** p <0.01, *** p <0.001.
[1] Scale: from 0 = None to 4 = three or more.
[2] Scale: from 1 = never to 4 = often.
[3] Scale: from 1 = no interaction to 4 = substantial interaction.
[4] Scale: from 1 = all or nearly all people of color to 5 = all or nearly all white.

and readings on the subject were significantly correlated with the end-of-year racial ideology, but when controlling for precollege racial ideology none of these measures was a significant predictor of ideology change. Perhaps precollege hierarchy-enhancing racial ideology leads students to avoid participation in the multicultural activities that precipitate hierarchy-attenuating racial ideologies.

Conversely, women and people of color had more significant predictors of racial ideology, which was a function of both more substantial changes during the first year in college, as well as having a higher number of survey respondents and therefore more variance to explain. As was the case with their white male counterparts, the frequency of discussions on race predicted a more hierarchy-attenuating racial ideology ($\beta = -.10*$). In addition, readings and materials on race/ethnicity had a similar impact ($\beta = -.14***$). However, having more white people in students' friendship groups ($\beta = 0.08*$) as well as an increased frequency of interactions with white students ($\beta = 0.07*$) both promoted a hierarchy-enhancing racial ideology.

Discussion of Mixed-Method and Intersectionality Approach

The preceding example demonstrates how a mixed-method intersectional analysis helped answer two questions: What is the dominant racial ideology of white male college students? What college experiences affect their development? The intersection of being white and being male was strongly related to subscribing to hierarchy-enhancing racial ideologies, which is in line with existing research (Sidanius and Pratto, 1999) and also makes intuitive sense. White men are the beneficiaries of both white privilege and male privilege (Feagin and O'Brien, 2003), and therefore they are also the ones whose ideological orientations support the hierarchical status quo (Sidanius and Pratto, 1999). They were also a group of students who were generally immune to influence in their racial ideologies during the first year of college. Aside from engaging in discussions about race, no other measures significantly affected racial ideology formation. Thus the college environment generally functioned as a reification of the racial status quo as it left these white male students insufficiently challenged ideologically regarding issues of race.

To the extent that ideology is a central component of the perpetuation of white supremacy (Bonilla-Silva, 2006), this analysis suggests that the collegiate environment served as an arena of racial stratification among the racially hyperprivileged. Within the campus environment specifically, the campus racial climate, or the beliefs, attitudes, and behaviors around issues of racial and ethnic diversity (Hurtado, Milem, Clayton-Pedersen, and Allen, 1999), cannot be improved without addressing the beliefs of those who perpetuate racist ideologies. Institutional researchers who are assessing climate often focus primarily on understanding the experiences and outcomes of those who are marginalized on college campuses, but strategies to improve campus environments and foster equity must also consider the ideologies, behaviors, and beliefs of those who are privileged. Institutional researchers can and should add a great deal to these efforts by not only assessing students' racial ideologies but also exploring strategies that appear to be effective in moving students from a hierarchy-enhancing to a more hierarchy-attenuating worldview.

Institutions of higher education have increasingly identified democratic outcomes (voting, civic engagement) and multicultural competence (perspective taking, ability to work in and with diverse groups, openness to new ideas) as necessary for success in today's diverse workforce and society (Engberg, 2007; Hurtado, 2006). To foster these outcomes on college and university campuses, it is important for institutional researchers to help institutional leaders and student affairs educators understand the beliefs that shape students' behaviors as they develop strategies that encourage engagement across difference and cross-cultural learning.

This study also has methodological implications for institutional researchers. Institutional research is frequently defined by large-scale surveys that measure student outcomes, and this is slightly at odds with intersectionality inquiries. As Hancock (2007a) argues, "the conventional wisdom among intersectionality scholars considers multiple methods necessary and sufficient" (p. 251). Thus the strengths of qualitative and quantitative approaches help compensate for the limitations of one another and generate more thorough analyses of structured inequality and individual or group experiences. For example, the interviews, though informative, were not able to resolve three issues: (1) if this construct was consistent across a larger population, (2) how white male racial ideologies related to the perspectives of nonwhite and female peers, and (3) what experiences during the first year of college affected racial ideology formation. The quantitative survey, however, helped address these limitations.

Although the survey instrument was not developed in direct response to data collected from the interviews, the similarity between the qualitative findings and survey constructs created an opportunity to compare students' racial ideologies on a larger scale. This suggests that much could be learned from data collected through a sequential exploratory design. Collecting interview or focus group data to develop theories and emerging patterns in higher education prior to survey can improve the accuracy and precision of quantitative findings, creating opportunities to test the validity of our perceptions about student development and campus experiences that students perceive as most central and salient.

Ultimately, the underlying questions guiding this research are prompted by a commitment to social justice. Institutional research often focuses on student-specific outcomes, with less consideration regarding what these outcomes mean in terms of the larger society. With respect to systemic racism, this analysis demonstrated that by leaving white male undergraduates insufficiently challenged regarding their racial selves during their first year of college, the institution inadvertently was helping perpetuate and support systemic racism. This analysis, however, can also be hopeful because institutional researchers following the methodology outlined in this research can play an integral role in identifying both how racism is perpetuated and how it can be challenged within colleges and universities.

References

Bonilla-Silva, E. *Racism Without Racists: Color-Blind Racism and the Persistence of Racial Inequality in the United States* (2nd ed.). Lanham, Md.: Rowman and Littlefield, 2006.

Bonilla-Silva, E., and Forman, T. E. "'I am not a racist but...': Mapping white college students' racial ideology in the USA." *Discourse & Society,* 2000, *11*(1), 50–85.

Bonilla-Silva, E., and Ray, V. "When Whites Love a Black Leader: Race Matters in Obamerica." *Journal of African American Studies,* 2009, *13*(2), 176–183.

Cabrera, N. L. *Invisible Racism: Male, Hegemonic Whiteness in Higher Education.* Unpublished doctoral dissertation. Los Angeles: University of California, Los Angeles, 2009.

College Board. *The Educational Crisis Facing Young Men of Color.* New York: College Board, 2010.

Crenshaw, K. W. "Mapping the Margins: Intersectionality, Identity Politics, and Violence Against Women of Color." In M. A. Fineman and R. Mykitiuk (eds.), *The Public Nature of Private Violence* (pp. 93–118). New York: Routledge, 1994.

Engberg, M. "Educating the Workforce for the 21st Century: A Cross-Disciplinary Analysis of the Impact of the Undergraduate Experience on Students' Development of a Pluralistic Orientation." *Research in Higher Education,* 2007, *48*(3), 283–317.

Evans, N. J., Forney, D. S., Guido, F. M., Renn, K. A., and Patton, L. D. *Student Development in College: Theory, Research, and Practice* (2nd ed.). San Francisco: Jossey-Bass, 2010.

Feagin, J. *Systemic Racism: A Theory of Oppression.* New York: Routledge, 2006.

Feagin, J., and O'Brien, E. *White Men on Race.* Boston: Beacon Press, 2003.

Hancock, A. M. "Intersectionalities as a Normative and Empirical Paradigm." *Politics and Gender,* 2007a, *3*(2), 248–254.

Hancock, A. M. "When Multiplication Doesn't Equal Quick Addition: Examining Intersectionality as a Research Paradigm." *Perspectives on Politics,* 2007b, *5*(1), 63–79.

Horowitz, D. "Speaker Responds to Wildcat." *Daily Wildcat* (2009, April 9). Retrieved from http://media.wildcat.arizona.edu/media/storage/paper997/news/2009/04/09/Opinions/Mail-Bag-3704213.shtml.

Hurtado, S. "Linking Diversity with the Educational and Civic Missions of Higher Education." *Review of Higher Education,* 2006, *30*(2), 185–196.

Hurtado, S., Milem, J., Clayton-Pedersen, A., and Allen, W. *Enacting Diverse Learning Environments: Improving the Climate for Racial/Ethnic Diversity in Higher Education.* Washington, D.C.: ASHE-ERIC Higher Education Report, 1999.

Omi, M. and Winant, H. *Racial Formation in the United States* (2nd ed). New York: Routledge, 1994.

Pierce, J. L. "'Racing for Innocence': Whiteness, Corporate Culture, and the Backlash Against Affirmative Action." In A. W. Doane and E. Bonilla-Silva (eds.), *White Out: The Continuing Significance of Racism* (pp. 199–214). New York: Routledge, 2003.

Regents of the University of California v. Bakke. 438 U.S. 312. 1978.

Riegle-Crumb, C. "More Girls Go to College: Exploring the Social and Academic Factors Behind the Female Postsecondary Advantage Among Hispanic and White Students." *Research in Higher Education,* 2010, *51*(6), 573–593.

Sáenz, V. B., and Ponjuan, L. "The Vanishing Latino Male in Higher Education." *Journal of Hispanic Higher Education,* 2009, *8*(1), 54–89.

Sidanius, J., and Pratto, F. *Social Dominance: An Intergroup Theory of Social Hierarchy and Oppression.* New York: Cambridge University Press, 1999.

Tashakkori, A., and Teddlie, C. *Handbook of Mixed-Methods in Social and Behavioral Research.* Thousand Oaks, Calif.: Sage, 2003.

Yin, R. K. *Case Study Research: Design and Methods* (2nd ed., vol. 5). Thousand Oaks, Calif.: Sage, 1994.

NOLAN L. CABRERA is an assistant professor of higher education at the University of Arizona in the Center for the Study of Higher Education.

7

In this chapter, the authors discuss the utility of using mixed-methods and intersectionality approaches to conducting research on campus climates and on sense of belonging.

The Utility of Using Mixed-Methods and Intersectionality Approaches in Conducting Research on Filipino American Students' Experiences with the Campus Climate and on Sense of Belonging

Dina C. Maramba, Samuel D. Museus

The campus climate—the current attitudes, perceptions, and expectations on a given campus—can have a profound influence on college students' experiences. For example, institutional climate, particularly around issues of race and ethnic diversity, has been statistically linked to student engagement, satisfaction, adjustment, persistence, and degree completion (Cabrera and others, 1999; Hurtado and Carter, 1997; Hurtado, Carter, and Spuler, 1996; Museus, Nichols, and Lambert, 2008; Nora and Cabrera, 1996). Importantly, campus climate can also influence the extent to which students feel they belong on their campus (Hurtado and Carter, 1997; Hurtado, Carter, and Spuler, 1996; Locks, Hurtado, Bowman, and Oseguera, 2008). If students feel they belong at their institution, they are more likely to succeed (Astin, 1975, 1984; Bean, 1980; Braxton, 2000; Braxton, Sullivan, and Johnson, 1997; Museus and Quaye, 2009; Tinto, 1987, 1993). It is therefore no surprise that many institutional leaders and researchers are concerned about whether their institutional climate fosters a sense of belonging among the undergraduate students whom they serve.

Unfortunately, there is a plethora of existing literature that highlights the fact that college students of color often encounter an unwelcoming campus climate (Hurtado, 1992; Harper and Hurtado, 2007; Museus and

NEW DIRECTIONS FOR INSTITUTIONAL RESEARCH, no. 151, Fall 2011 © Wiley Periodicals, Inc.
Published online in Wiley Online Library (wileyonlinelibrary.com) • DOI: 10.1002/ir.401

Truong, 2009). A small body of research also indicates that Filipino American college students, specifically, encounter challenges navigating the environment of their campus (Maramba, 2008; Maramba and Museus, forthcoming; Museus and Maramba, 2011). These inquiries, however, are sparse, and there is little understanding of how race, ethnicity, gender, and other aspects of Filipino American students' identities shape their experiences and perceptions of the campus climate.

In the remainder of this chapter, we discuss how merging mixed-methods and intersectional analyses can generate deeper and more authentic understandings of students' experiences within the campus climate and its relation to sense of belonging in college. In the following section, we discuss overemphasis on one-dimensional analyses of campus climates and sense of belonging, emphasizing the importance of considering students' multiple identities in campus climate research and assessment. Then we discuss a mixed-methods intersectional analysis of campus climates and sense of belonging. In doing so, we highlight how the mixed-methods and intersectional approach helped uncover understandings that solely quantitative, exclusively qualitative, or one-dimensional analyses could not generate.

Mixed-Methods and Intersectionality in Conducting Research on Campus Climates and Sense of Belonging

When researchers seek to understand campus climates, they often conduct quantitative analyses, comparing racial groups' perceptions of and experiences within the campus climate. Researchers have also engaged in qualitative examinations that highlight how racial populations experience the climate of their campus (for a comprehensive discussion of climate research, see Harper and Hurtado, 2007).

Although such approaches help generate an understanding of how perceptions of climate differ and how they shape the experiences of college students, these analytic strategies are also limited in many ways. For example, quantitative inquiries typically compare the perceptions and experiences of two or more racial groups, while failing to further disaggregate. They rarely take into account how multiple aspects of students' identities shape their perceptions and experiences. Further, qualitative inquiries provide in-depth descriptions regarding how students experience campus climates, but they can fail to examine how that deeper understanding informs knowledge of larger student populations. By using mixed methods, researchers can incorporate the strengths of both quantitative and qualitative methods into their research and assessment designs. As we demonstrate in the next sections, collecting and analyzing both quantitative and qualitative data can complement one another in a way that generates a unique and authentic picture of students' experiences within the climate of their campus.

NEW DIRECTIONS FOR INSTITUTIONAL RESEARCH • DOI: 10.1002/ir

Just as mono-method studies are limited in their utility in research on campus climates and sense of belonging, overemphasis on a singular dimension of students' identities can also limit the understandings generated by climate and sense of belonging studies. Research on campus climates and sense of belonging typically focuses on illuminating differences between students' perceptions and experiences by race (Cabrera and others, 1999; Harper and Hurtado, 2007; Hurtado and Carter, 1997; Hurtado, Carter, and Spuler, 1996; Museus, Nichols, and Lambert, 2008; Nora and Cabrera, 1996). It has been noted, however, that significant variation in perceptions of and experiences with the campus climate can exist within a racial group (Museus and Truong, 2009). Moreover, researchers have noted that gender influences the ways in which students experience the campus climate, yet this reality is often ignored in research on climate and sense of belonging (Maramba, 2008). Given this reality, it behooves individuals who are conducting campus climate research and assessment to consider how race and gender might mutually shape students' experiences and sense of belonging. The investigation described here constitutes an example of how such consideration of multiple intersecting identities can generate more complex and authentic understandings of experiences with institutional climates and sense of belonging in higher education.

Example of a Mixed-Methods Intersectional Analysis of Filipino American Students' Experiences with the Campus Climate and Sense of Belonging

In this section, we discuss the process by which we conducted a mixed-methods intersectional analysis of Filipino American students' experiences with the campus climate and their sense of belonging. The initial analysis was focused on understanding how race and gender influence students' experiences in the campus climates and sense of belonging. The mixed-methods nature of the analysis led to a post hoc analysis that uncovered realities masked in the initial study.

Phase I: Defining the Purpose. The purpose of the inquiry was to understand how race and gender influence Filipino students' experiences in the campus climate and sense of belonging in college. Specifically, we sought to understand whether there were differences in experiences with the campus climate and sense of belonging across female and male Filipino students at one large, public, racially diverse, urban research university.

Phase II: Selecting the Approach. After considering the various mixed-methods approaches (see Chapter Two for discussion), we selected a triangulation mixed-method design. This refers to designs in which different but complementary data are collected on the same topic (Creswell and Plano Clark, 2007). Also, the qualitative and quantitative phases of the study are often conducted concurrently in triangulation designs, with findings being integrated at the interpretation stage of the inquiry.

Phase III: Creating the Instruments. The survey was constructed using items from preexisting surveys. The instrument included demographic questions, a university environment scale (Gloria and Kurpius, 1996), sense of belonging scale (Hurtado and Carter, 1997), campus racial climate scale (Hurtado, 1992), and several other items measuring constructs such as self-esteem and family environment. For the purposes of this example, we focus on students' demographics, an item about hostility of the campus racial climate, and the sense of belonging scale. Demographic variables included in the analysis were gender and class level (first, second, third, or fourth year). The hostile campus racial climate survey item measured the degree to which students agreed with the statement "There is a lot of campus racial conflict here." The campus racial climate item was measured on a Likert scale with four values: (1) strongly disagree, (2) disagree, (3) agree, and (4) strongly agree. Survey items measuring sense of belonging asked participants to indicate how strongly they agreed with the statements (1) I see myself as part of the campus community, (2) I feel that I am a member of the campus community, (3) I feel a sense of belonging to the campus community. Responses to these three questions were also measured on a Likert scale with the four values listed above, ranging from strongly agree to strongly disagree. These three items were used to create a composite, continuous sense of belonging scale.

The interview protocol was developed to reflect the constructs that were included in the aforementioned survey. For example, with regard to sense of belonging, the protocol included the questions (1) What are your overall perceptions of your campus experience and campus climate (academically and socially)? (2) Can you describe the challenges to feeling a sense of belonging at your campus? And, (3) What has been helpful in feeling a sense of belonging in college?

Phase IV: Collecting the Data. For the quantitative component of the inquiry, four hundred questionnaires were distributed to approximately 40 percent of the Filipino American student population on the participating campus. A total of 143 participants returned the survey, resulting in a 36 percent response rate. Fifty-seven percent of respondents were women and 43 percent were men. Thirty-nine percent of respondents were first- and second-year students, and 61 percent of respondents were third- and fourth-year students.

Survey participants were subsequently contacted and asked to participate in individual interviews, and thirty-eight students agreed to do so. Fifty-eight percent of interview participants were women, 42 percent men. Thirty-two percent of interview participants were first- or second-year students; 68 percent were third- and fourth-year undergraduates.

Phase V: Analyzing the Data. Because of the categorical nature of hostile campus racial climate item, a Pearson's chi-square test was used to analyze the quantitative data, assessing whether a relationship existed between gender and perceived hostility of the climate. In addition, we analyzed the continuous sense of belonging scale using independent samples t-tests to determine whether differences existed by gender.

To analyze the qualitative data, we used constant comparative techniques with research notes, observations and transcriptions from the interviews (Strauss and Corbin, 1998). In constant comparative analysis, the researcher engages in a process of collecting and analyzing the data simultaneously during each stage of data collection (Jones, Torres, and Arminio, 2006). Analyzing and interpreting at each part of the process results in being able to identify codes (Jones, Torres, and Arminio, 2006). We used open-coding techniques, which involved analyzing the data line by line, to generate themes from the data (Straus and Corbin, 1998). We continued with this process until the data became redundant or reached a saturation point (Bogdan and Biklen, 1998). Finally, we incorporated memo writing to further refine and enhance our themed categories and understanding how they relate to each other.

Phase VI: Generating the Findings. The chi-square test indicated that there was no relationship between gender and perceived hostility of the campus climate ($p = .86$), and the t-test results also indicated no statistically significant difference in sense of belonging between men and women at the .05 level of significance (male $x = 8.52$, female $x = 8.00$, $p = .09$). With regard to the qualitative findings, three main themes emerged from the data: students experienced (1) a lack of belonging at the institution, (2) a lack of voice on campus, and (3) hostile classroom climates.

Lack of Belonging. Participants' reported experiencing a lack of belonging at some point in their college career, and they sought and became involved in student organizations on campus to address that lack of belonging. There were differences in how female and male students talked about their sense of belonging and involvement. Women in the study often discussed *how they felt* before their involvement in the student organizations. Descriptions included that they felt they "did not belong here," "needed to drop out," and "always felt isolated." In contrast to women, men talked about what they *needed to do* to feel a sense of belonging on campus. For example, one man said, "I do belong here" and "I just need to find it" (where he belongs, referring specifically to student organizations).

Feeling Voiceless on Campus. Related to the lack of belonging, students reported feeling voiceless on campus. All of the participants spoke of not having a voice within the campus environment. A number of them shared that they did not feel well represented on campus as Filipino Americans, because of their low representation among students, faculty, and administrators. Although both men and women reported feeling voiceless in the campus environment, women also reported feeling voiceless within their family environment.

Hostile Classroom Climates. Students indicated that another reason they experienced a lack of belonging on campus was hostile classroom environments. All of the participants shared negative and awkward inter-actions with their professors and teaching assistants. Even though both men and women spoke of negative exchanges in the classroom, there were very subtle differences in the *types* of negative interactions within the classroom environment. Whereas men often spoke of being directly "shot down" by professors and teaching assistants for ideas that they may share in class, women reported often feeling that their ideas were dismissed or "not heard."

The findings of the quantitative and qualitative analyses conflicted, with the former indicating that there were no differences in students' sense of belonging and the latter suggesting there were variations in how men and women conceptualized sense of belonging. The men in the study seemed to view their lack of belonging on campus with greater hope to fit in and a more proactive philosophy and focusing on what they needed to do in order to find a sense of belonging on campus. It is possible that this hopeful and proactive approach was associated with the fact that those men had a home environment where they experienced having a voice.

Despite both men and women in the sample indicating that they experienced a lack of belonging on campus, the subtle gender differences that emerged in the qualitative analysis led us to question whether male students in the sample were eventually better able to adjust to the environ-ments of the campus and find a sense of belonging than their female coun-terparts. The survey data were not longitudinal and were therefore not ideal for answering this question, but we determined that we could get some sense of whether men appeared to achieve greater sense of belonging in the later years of college by taking into account not only gender but also the student's year in college.

Phase VII: Conducting the Post Hoc Analysis. To explore whether men were more likely to experience a lack of belonging on campus, we disaggregated the overall sample into two subsamples: (1) first-year stu-dents and sophomores, and (2) juniors and seniors. Again, independent t-tests were used to determine whether there were gender differences in sense of belonging for each of the two subsamples. Interestingly, the results indicated that female first-year students and sophomores reported a slightly higher level of belonging than their male peers but the gender dif-ference was insignificant (male $x = 8.54$, female $x = 8.68$, $p = 0.79$). In con-trast, and congruent with our suspicion, the findings also suggest that male juniors and seniors reported a greater sense of belonging than their female counterparts, and the differences were statistically significant at the .05 level (male $x = 8.50$, female $x = 7.55$, $p = 0.01$).

In sum, the initial quantitative findings revealed no relationship between gender and perceived hostility of the racial climate or sense of belonging. The qualitative findings, however, indicated there were nuanced differences that helped us rethink how we analyzed the quantitative data, and this led to a post hoc quantitative analysis that accounted for class level and revealed a more complex picture, including a relationship between gender and sense of belonging among an upper-class subsample.

The mixed-methods and intersectionality approaches generated a more holistic and accurate picture of the relationship among gender, campus climate, and sense of belonging than would have emerged from using mono-methods techniques. In addition, the mixed-methods intersectional analysis could have critical implications for how college educators mentor and develop programs for Filipino men and women.

Lessons Learned from the Inquiry

We conclude with a few lessons learned from the inquiry. These lessons can inform the work of scholars and institutional researchers who plan to conduct research on campus climates and sense of belonging.

Do Not Rely on Aggregated Data. In the preceding example, quantitative analysis of the aggregated sample failed to generate an accurate understanding of gender differences. Aggregated analysis can often be misleading because it masks critical differences across subpopulations (see Chapter One for more in-depth discussion). Scholars and institutional researchers should consider the various ways in which their data can be disaggregated to generate the most accurate picture of the individuals, groups, processes, organizations, or phenomena they are studying.

Use Qualitative Data to Conceptualize Quantitative Research. When considering mixed-methods research, it is easy to think about how quantitative and qualitative methods can generate unique findings or how one method can be used to generate instruments used in the other. However, the preceding example provides a glimpse of how researchers can use the nuances found via qualitative methods to rethink making decisions on disaggregating data, designing quantitative analyses, and redesigning those examinations.

Keep in Mind the Multiple Purposes of Mixed-Methods Approaches. The preceding inquiry began as a concurrent, triangulation mixed-methods inquiry that was focused on using quantitative and qualitative methods to complement each other. However, the conflict between the findings of the two approaches led to a subsequent quantitative analysis, resulting in the examination exhibiting some of the characteristics of sequential exploratory design, in which qualitative analyses help researchers design and conceptualize the quantitative component. Scholars and institutional researchers should maintain flexibility and use the combination(s) of methods that can most effectively answer the research questions they ask.

References

Astin, A. W. *Preventing Students from Dropping Out.* San Francisco: Jossey-Bass, 1975.

Astin, A. W. "Student Involvement: A Developmental Theory for Higher Education." *Journal of College Student Personnel*, 1984, 25(4), 297–308.

Bean, J. "Dropouts and Turnover: The Synthesis and Test of a Casual Model of Student Attrition." *Research in Higher Education*, 1980, 12(2), 155–187.

Bogdan, R. C, and Biklen, S. K. *Qualitative Research for Education: An Introduction to Theory and Methods* (3rd ed.). Boston: Allyn and Bacon, 1998.

Braxton, J. M. "Reinvigorating Theory and Research on the Departure Puzzle." In J. M. Braxton (ed.) *Reworking the Student Departure Puzzle* (pp. 257–274) Nashville, Tenn.: Vanderbilt University Press, 2000.

Braxton, J. M., Sullivan, A. V., and Johnson, R. M. "Appraising Tinto's Theory of College Student Departure." In J. C. Smart (ed.), *Higher Education: Handbook of Theory and Research* (vol. 12). New York: Agathon Press, 1997.

Cabrera, A., Nora, A., Pascarella, E. T., Terenzini, P. T., and Hagedorn, L. "Campus Racial Climate and the Adjustment of Students to College: A Comparison Between White Students and African-American Students." *Journal of Higher Education*, 1999, 70, 134–160.

Creswell, J. W., and Plano Clark, V. L. *Designing and Conducting Mixed-Methods Research*. Thousand Oaks, Calif.: Sage, 2007.

Gloria, A. M., and Kurpius, S.E.R. "The Validation of the Cultural Congruity Scale and the University Environment Scale with Chicano/a Students." *Hispanic Journal of Behavioral Sciences*, 1996, 18(4), 533–549.

Harper, S., and Hurtado, S. "Nine Themes in Campus Racial Climates and Implications for Institutional Transformation." In S. Harper and L. Patton (eds.), *Responding to the Realities of Race on College Campuses*. New Directions for Student Services, no. 120. San Francisco: Jossey-Bass, 2007.

Hurtado, S. "The Campus Racial Climate: Contexts of Conflict." *Journal of Higher Education*, 1992, 63(5), 539–569.

Hurtado, S., and Carter, D. "Effects of College Transition and Perceptions of the Campus Racial Climate on Latina/o College Students' Sense of Belonging." *Sociology of Education*, 1997, 70, 324–345.

Hurtado, S., Carter, D., and Spuler, A. "Latino Student Transition to College: Assessing Difficulties and Factors in Successful College Adjustment." *Research in Higher Education*, 1996, 37, 135–157.

Jones, S. R., Torres, V., and Arminio, J. *Negotiating the Complexities of Qualitative Research in Higher Education*. New York: Routledge, 2006.

Locks, A. M., Hurtado, S., Bowman, N. A., and Oseguera, L. "Extending Notions of Campus Climate and Diversity to Students' Transition to College. *The Review of Higher Education*, 2008, 31(3), 257–285.

Maramba, D. C. "Understanding Campus Climate Through the Voices of Filipina/o American College Students." *College Student Journal*, 2008, 42(4), 1045–1060.

Maramba, D. C., and Museus, S. D. "Examining the Effects of Campus Climate, Ethnic Group Cohesion and Cross Cultural Interaction on Filipino American Students' Sense of Belonging in College." *Journal of College Student Retention*, forthcoming.

Museus, S. D., and Maramba, D. C. "The Impact of Culture on Filipino American Students' Sense of Belonging." *Review of Higher Education*, 2011, 34(2), 231–258.

Museus, S. D., Nichols, A. H., and Lambert, A. "Racial Differences in the Effects of Campus Racial Climate on Degree Completion: A Structural Model." *Review of Higher Education*, 2008, 32(1), 107–134.

Museus, S. D., and Quaye, S. J. "Toward an Intercultural Perspective of Racial and Ethnic Minority College Student Persistence." *Review of Higher Education*, 2009, 33(1), 67–94.

Museus, S. D., and Truong, K. A. "Disaggregating Qualitative Data on Asian Americans in Campus Climate Research and Assessment." In S. D. Museus (ed.), *Conducting Research on Asian Americans in Higher Education*. New Directions for Institutional Research, no. 142, pp. 17–26. San Francisco: Jossey-Bass, 2009.

Nora, A., and Cabrera, A. "The Role of Perceptions of Prejudice and Discrimination on the Adjustment of Minority Students to College." *Journal of Higher Education*, 1996, 67, 119–148.

Strauss, A., and Corbin, J. *Basics of Qualitative Research: Techniques and Procedures for Developing Grounded Theory* (2nd ed.). Thousand Oaks, Calif.: Sage, 1998.

Tinto, V. *Leaving College: Rethinking the Causes and Cures of Student Attrition.* Chicago: University of Chicago Press, 1987.

Tinto, V. *Leaving College: Rethinking the Causes and Cures of Student Attrition* (2nd ed.). Chicago: University of Chicago Press, 1993.

DINA C. MARAMBA is an assistant professor of student affairs administration and Asian and Asian American Studies at the State University of New York (SUNY), Binghamton.

SAMUEL D. MUSEUS is an assistant professor of educational administration at the University of Hawai'i Manoa.

8

This chapter explores how mixed-methods research can reveal a more complex understanding of students' conceptualizations of their own identities.

Identity, Intersectionality, and Mixed-Methods Approaches

Casandra E. Harper

As higher education serves an increasingly diverse student population, efforts to understand and account for that diversity have evolved, particularly within theories describing students' identities (race, gender, class, religion, etc.) and how they develop over the span of college (Evans and others, 2010). Although most identity theories focus on one dimension at a time—such as women's identity (Josselson, 1996) or African American identity (Cross, 1991)—some recent theories account for how identities intersect simultaneously and are interdependent (Abes, Jones, and McEwen, 2007; Jones and McEwen, 2000; Reynolds and Pope, 1991). Applying this intersectionality perspective to students' identities can provide a more nuanced and holistic view of those individuals. The challenge, however, in this approach also raises issues within the contexts of research and practice (Bowleg, 2008; Stewart, 2010), including uncertainties around how institutional researchers can accurately capture, measure, and assess students' intersecting identities.

In this chapter, I argue that current strategies to study and understand students' identities fall short of fully capturing their complexity. A multidimensional perspective and a mixed-methods approach can reveal nuance that is missed with current approaches. In the following sections, I offer an illustration of how mixed-methods research can promote a more nuanced understanding of how students perceive their identity. Further, I highlight the ways in which intersectionality and mixed methods can inform seemingly one-dimensional categories, such as race, as well as

NEW DIRECTIONS FOR INSTITUTIONAL RESEARCH, no. 151, Fall 2011 © Wiley Periodicals, Inc.
Published online in Wiley Online Library (wileyonlinelibrary.com) • DOI: 10.1002/ir.402

identity more broadly defined, where all salient characteristics (race, gender, class) are considered simultaneously. Finally, I conclude the chapter with a discussion of application of these ideas to practice within the context of institutional research.

Research and Methodological Approaches to Capturing Identity

Methodological concerns often materialize when considering how to numerically represent the presence of various groups on college and university campuses. How we count individuals has implications for policy, practice, and individual lives. Cohen (1982) found that historically "the activity of counting and measuring itself altered the way people thought about what they were quantifying: numeracy could be an agent of change" (p. 206). The methodological challenge of capturing identity applies to multiple individual dimensions of students, such as gender, race, major, class, religion, political orientation, and sexual orientation. Students are dynamic beings, and their identity dimensions sometimes shift over the span of college and are therefore not as clear and static as we often assume they are in higher education. For example, students' demographic information might be assessed for institutional purposes on an admissions application, and those data might be drawn on for the remainder of the student's tenure at that institution even though his or her identity preferences may change. Even in the case where new data are collected while a student is in college, changes in that student's identity characteristics are not often compared from one survey to another.

The identity dimension that receives the most attention, in terms of regulation and categorical changes, is race. The variability in capturing and counting racial background creates unique methodological opportunities and challenges for institutional research, and it constitutes a useful illustration of the intersectionality of identity. Colleges and universities are directed by the U.S. Department of Education on racial collection and dissemination standards that are compliant with the Office of Management and Budget (OMB). Some research indicates that institutions are slow to make changes to comply, and some are not in compliance with these mandates (Padilla and Kelley, 2005; Renn and Lunceford, 2004). The most recent standards (see "Final Guidance on Maintaining, Collecting, and Reporting Racial and Ethnic Data to the U.S. Department of Education," 2007), call for institutions to report ethnic and racial data according to nine categories: (1) Hispanic/Latino, regardless of race; (2) American Indian or Alaska Native; (3) Asian; (4) Black or African American; (5) Native Hawaiian or Other Pacific Islander; (6) White; (7) two or more races; (8) unknown; and (9) nonresident alien. These standards have implications for how racial and ethnic data are collected, coded, and reported across all levels of an institution. Compliance with these standards requires mass coordination efforts, revision of all paper and electronic forms and surveys, and strategies to update or compare existing data with the new format (Cohen, Fink, Conley, and Sapp, 2008).

Regardless of the catalyst behind changes in racial categories or the imperfection of the categories themselves, the survey or checklist approach may very well be the best option available to capture students' racial identities. Nevertheless, we should be cognizant of the weaknesses involved in capturing race on surveys since these devices do not get at the complexity of students' racial identities and realities. Racial self-categorization is susceptible to issues of survey design (Morning, 2002), wording of the categories used (Bayer, 1972–73), delivery format (written or verbal; Harper, 2007), setting and presence of others (Harris and Sim, 2002), and the perceived consequences of the choice (Harper, 2007). Further, students' responses to categorization will vary (Bowleg, 2008). For example, a student might consistently mark the same category when asked multiple times, but the meaning the student attributes to that category might change. We must question the degree to which these categories differ from students' sense of who they are and their backgrounds.

The challenges associated with collecting data on students' racial and ethnic identities become particularly salient when discussing mixed race or multiracial college students. For example, a recent national and longitudinal study of 1,101 students who identified as "multiracial" revealed that the majority (66 percent) marked only one race to describe themselves when they entered college, whereas a majority (56 percent) marked two or more races to describe their background during their senior year (Harper, 2007). Thus the quantitative analyses revealed a large shift in the number of students who changed how they identified themselves racially over their time in college. There are three striking implications of this finding. First, if racial data were collected only during the first year in college, the majority of these students would be classified according to a single race despite most marking more than one category during their senior year. Second, if the longitudinal approach had not been taken, the wide shifts in the number of students going from marking one category as freshmen to more than one as seniors, or vice versa, would have been missed, to say nothing of the additional shifts in which categories were marked. Third, this raises the question of whether other identity dimensions, such as class, gender, or religion, are similarly dynamic but are treated as being static.

Capturing multiracial students within institutional data is a difficult charge because "accuracy" is a moving target, subject to politics, context, and the social construction of race (Harper, 2007). The attempt to capture fluid, dynamic, and multidimensional constructs—such as race—with static, unchanging, one-dimensional categories is problematic because it does not fully address the meaning students associate with those categories. Students could respond to a racial background question by simultaneously (1) considering which racial categories are present and which are absent, (2) reading the notes next to certain categories describing the groups or countries considered as part of that category, (3) working within the guidelines indicated in the wording of the question, and (4) using all of these clues to detect the paradigm of race being presented at the time. For example, the aforementioned racial and ethnic data collection standards require Hispanic/Latino students to be classified as such regardless of their racial background. This is likely a much different view of race than those with which these students are familiar, since these guidelines mandate that Hispanic/Latino students be classified as not having a race. If students comply with the OMB standards and ignore their own racial background, is that more accurate than maintaining their own identification preferences? Is a response based on familial or biological connections more accurate than one based on cultural affinity?

Perhaps colleges can avoid relying solely on data collected from the politically charged context of the college application and draw from institutional research surveys, which are not completely removed from politics either but do promise students individual anonymity and have fewer direct consequences for students. If they take this approach and students' categorization of their race during freshman and senior year differ, is the freshman response more or less accurate than the designation as a senior? If the question also asks about parental race and the presence of that question limits or alters how students designate their own background, or if the selection the student makes for himself or herself does not neatly comprise mother's and father's race, which is the accurate reflection of the student's background? How should parental race be taken into account when summarizing the racial background of the student?

Even if institutions attempt to abandon written conceptualizations of race and personalize their approach by verbally asking students about their background, the race and perceived motivation of the people asking those questions might alter participants' responses. The students' responses could vary according to their particular feelings on that day or at that moment. If students do not see race as independent of other constructs, such as gender, can racial background be accurately portrayed without also reporting gender?

Taking a more complex, multidimensional view of identity by using an intersectional and mixed-methods approach helps avoid some of the reductive consequences of current approaches. Using multiple strategies to capture and report students' identity may add greater complexity and clarity about the multiple dimensions of students' identity and how these dimensions intersect. Examining the intersectional nature of identity using a mixed-methods approach offers an opportunity to gain new understandings of variation in students' responses over time or across contexts. Mixed-methods designs offer an opportunity to reconcile the perspectives gleaned by using different methods (Creswell, 2009). This approach can also reveal changes in the *meaning* that students attribute to quantitative conceptualizations of identity, even when those choices appear to remain unchanged.

Mixed Methods and Institutional Research

Institutional researchers are charged with responsibility for capturing and disseminating key information about students. Strategies to fulfill this responsibility can vary; attention has been paid to the benefits and drawbacks of various approaches and their ability to inform decision-making processes (Howard and Borland, 2001). For example, quantitative approaches to studying intersectionality are flawed and are arguably incompatible with the underlying assumptions of intersectionality (Shields, 2008). Quantitative research might examine the interaction of one identity dimension in comparison to another, as with race and gender, but such an approach is inadequate because it assumes independence of these categories and tends to "settle for identification of points of mutual effect without appreciation of the dependence of one category's very definition on the other and vice versa" (Shields, 2008, p. 306). This view is distinct from intersectionality, which views identity in multiplicative terms, where identities are co-constructed and inherently interdependent (Bowleg, 2008; Nash, 2008). There is also the added concern that quantitative approaches perpetuate categorization and oversimplification of students' identities and cannot fully capture the complexity within and across identity constructs (Diamond and Butterworth, 2008; Shields, 2008).

Qualitative methods have been viewed as being "more compatible with the theoretical language and intent of intersectionality" (Shields, 2008, p. 306), and mixed-methods approaches are arguably most preferred, though many have grappled with this issue and found no methodological solutions or clear processes to follow. McCall (2005) reviewed the prevailing approaches to intersectionality in research and finds that they fall on a spectrum ranging from rejecting categories to using them strategically. McCall identifies a blended approach of questioning categories while examining "particular social groups at neglected points of intersection" (p. 1774), or identities at the borders of group membership.

Integrating quantitative and qualitative approaches yields a more complete contextual understanding of an issue, which is needed to inform policy and practice (Perkins, 2001). Mixed-methods research reveals the complexity of identity in two main ways: (1) it can add understanding of how students might conceptualize a single categorical identity (such as race) dimension using multiple categories (race, ethnicity, gender, culture), and (2) it can reveal changes, development, and nuance to what might first appear static and simplistic. To illustrate these ideas, I draw from a mixed-methods study I conducted that examined the racial identification patterns, longitudinally and across contexts, of mixed-race college students. Even though my focus was race, other identity dimensions emerged as being relevant to students' understanding of their own racial identity.

As previously mentioned, the quantitative results revealed changes in 1,101 students' identity choices over the span of their time in college, as well as the individual and institutional variables associated with the odds of changing toward or maintaining the decision to mark more than one race as a senior. These analyses revealed the importance of variables such as joining a racial or ethnic student organization, having divorced parents, moving to a new state for college, living on campus, discussing politics, changing views toward affirmative action, and satisfaction with the relevance of coursework to everyday life. Since longitudinal changes to racial identity questions among college students are understudied, these results revealed previously unexplored variables associated with specific choices. Some of the predictors were counterintuitive or significant for more than one designation pattern, making it necessary to understand the experiences and meaning associated with these results from a qualitative perspective.

The purpose of the qualitative component of the study was to elicit a descriptive portrait of the meaning behind the racial and ethnic identification choices of a campus-specific sample of ten mixed-race college students and to identify, via sixty- to ninety-minute interviews, students' thoughts about these complex concepts of race, ethnicity, and identity. I questioned participants about specific contexts in which they might be asked about their background to get a sense of their responses across a range of contexts a student could typically face during his or her time in college. The purpose of this line of questions was to discover whether the responses would change in verbal versus written contexts or in situations with a varying level of personal anonymity and consequences.

Specifically, participants were asked (and in the following order) how they would answer if they were responding to (1) a stranger, (2) the U.S. Census (as constructed in 2000), (3) an anonymous consumer satisfaction survey, (4) their college roommate(s), (5) their college application, (6) the Higher Education Research Institute's Freshman Survey, and (7) the Higher Education Research Institute's College Student Survey (also referred to as the CSS, administered to graduating seniors). I attempted to link each of these contexts to actual events, asking participants to reflect on their own experience and if they could recall their response. For the written contexts, I offered participants full-color photocopies of the original documents and asked them to answer the racial background questions. The results revealed overlapping constructions of race, ethnicity, identity, and culture. The examples given here are drawn from the interview data and illustrate the intersectionality of identity.

Ethnicity and Generational Status. In verbally responding to questions about students' racial identity, some participants discussed self-identifying as "American" but having to amend that answer to appease others. Responding to people's inquiries with "I'm American" is never satisfying; nor is it ever enough of an answer. Several students believe their racial identity always requires elaboration. According to one participant, named Kaya, the reason for this was that if a person detects that something about a multiracial person's appearance is not purely white, they want to know what the nonwhite part is and will ask, "Oh, no, what are you really?" or "What's your ethnicity?" Kaya expressed feeling frustrated by the "What are you?" question:

> Even though I'm mostly Chinese, I'm third and fourth generation; on one side maybe like 19th, 20th [generation], I don't know. So I'm really American but people are not satisfied with that answer, so I just, after a while I'm just like, you know what, just give them what they want and then they'll stop bothering you. And if they want to talk about race I'll go ahead and talk about race but as it is, it's just really frustrating.

These comments about an American identity highlight the complex interconnection among race, ethnicity, nationality, and culture. Kaya identified generational status as being an issue in relating to other Chinese students on campus, many of whom she identified as second-generation, fluent in Chinese, and having a different set of experiences from her own. The students thought about these concepts using overlapping terms, which creates some difficulty in trying to capture the full extent of their background in the various ways they chose to express it. Current approaches to racial and ethnic categorization in higher education would miss this students' preference to identify as American; the students' Chinese heritage would likely be captured, though the generational history of that heritage would almost certainly be missed.

Students' Race, Parental Race, and Gender. Another approach to understanding students' own racial backgrounds is to ask about the racial background of students' parents. This option was particularly appealing to Kaya. She found that parental race increased the accuracy of information about her racial identity because "it makes a big difference where your parents came from," as well as which parent had which racial background. In her opinion, "Some people look down on it if your father is white and your mother is Asian." Kaya also did not think it would change what she marked for herself but thought it could have done so theoretically, because of the increased level of accuracy in her own racial background by having parental race accounted for:

> I mean I could mark something else because it's more clear for my mother and father now. It's more accurate because I can clearly define my ethnic background, including possible sexual/social cultural differences as they relate to the races of my parents. I can also show more clearly that I am not just half something and half something else. I think the fact that I am mostly

[Chinese] makes a difference in how people have responded to me in my life and thus shaped who I've become.

Kaya is noting two levels of clarity offered by parental race. First, it adds specificity to the racial background of each parent, which she finds crucial because of the sociological implications not just of race but of race when it intersects with gender. Second, in her eyes it is a quantitatively more accurate representation of her background because, without parental race, she is bothered by the fact that it is implied she is exactly half-Asian and half-white when she marks both categories.

Another participant, Maria, considered the parental race question "interesting" and thought of the implications for the statistics that would be reported using these data. She noted that the researchers compiling the data would have to "figure out how they want to count you, what your father is, what your mother is, how they want to count you despite . . . what you put." This comment reveals an understanding about the complicated nature of data and the flexibility that exists among researchers to manipulate or transform the data for reasons that may not be related to an individual's identification preferences. All participants, at one or more points in their interview, expressed lack of clarity about how their racial and ethnic responses would be compiled or reported, and this was certainly true with respect to the addition of parental race.

Race, Ethnicity, and Country of Origin. Another participant, José, was born and raised in Honduras. He offered an interesting perspective of how race and ethnicity are constructed in this country and how pervasive their influence is, certainly within the context of higher education: "I'm racially black, but here in the U.S. because I'm coming from a different country and I have different cultural norms, I speak Spanish; people may not associate me being African American or black, simply because of that. So that's a social construct right there." He finds that his daily interactions with new people reveal their preconceived notions about what it means to be black, because they are surprised when they hear his Spanish accent "and then they say, 'so you're not black then.' That's a social construction."

In his first week in the United States, one of the initial things he learned, even before learning English, was a lesson in the social construction of race. He received help from a citizenship center that is primarily focused on the needs of the Latino community. Despite José personally identifying as black, the person he received help from told him to mark "Latino" because of where he was born. Two years later, when he applied to college in the United States, he marked more than one category: "African American/black" and "other Spanish," specifying with a write-in response that he is "Honduran." Within other contexts, he is intentional about the boxes he marks and says that it "always depends on what I'm applying for." For example, when applying for the Hispanic Scholarship Fund, race and ethnicity were combined and the categories were based on

NEW DIRECTIONS FOR INSTITUTIONAL RESEARCH • DOI: 10.1002/ir

geography and place of birth, so he checked the "Hispanic" box for that. "If it's a scholarship for African Americans, I check black. It all depends on where I am and what I'm doing. Sometimes you can check more than one, so I put both, black and Latino." Overall, he notes that he has always felt black, but when he came to the United States people perceived him differently, not because of skin color but because of his country of origin. Because of this, and because of how race and ethnicity are constructed in the United States, he has adopted a Latino ethnic identity because of his "cultural background, traditions, and food," which are Latin American.

Current approaches to capturing race and ethnicity in higher education first ask students to identify their "ethnicity," which is represented as a dichotomy of being Hispanic/Latino or not, and students who are not Hispanic/Latino are then asked to indicate a "race." José indicated he would identify ethnically as Latino, but his primary identity has always been his black racial identity, which is missed under the current OMB guidelines for racial data collection. If researchers were to pursue in-person, visual accounts of José's race rather than surveys, they would classify him as black, which is aligned with his own racial self-identification, but they would likely be unaware of his cultural and ethnic identity.

Each of these examples reveals the intersectionality of identity and how qualitative research can be used to understand the complex issues related to quantitative inquiries about students' identities, and used to uncover nuance and complexity within seemingly one-dimensional, static categories. This discussion raises a number of issues, however, regarding our ability to capture identity accurately and the implications this will have for individuals. The next section addresses the methodological and practical challenges associated with capturing the intersectionality of students' identities.

Capturing Multidimensional Identity in Research and Practice

In this final section, I offer practical implications of using mixed-methods to study the intersectional nature of identity. Using more than one strategy for capturing dimensions of identity would add greater complexity but perhaps add clarity to current conceptualizations of identity and the extent to which students differ in their designation choices over time and across contexts. If these differences are discussed among individuals seeking the information and among respondents, this clarity might produce interesting and valuable discussions about dimensions of identity. Although institutional priorities in data collection and reporting might be to simplify and aggregate students into broadly accepted categories, there may also be opportunities to take a disaggregated and perhaps atypical approach to racial categorization. In doing so, we might challenge the current categories and how they serve to oversimplify identity.

As illustrated in the previous section, accuracy of racial categorization is a moving target and depends on one's perspective. From the viewpoint of the institution, accuracy might mean comparability with previous or existing data and conforming to existing practices and guidelines. For students, accuracy might consist of recognition of identity development and personal preferences. This latter perspective could lead to multiple forms of data collection, as well as multiple reporting and dissemination strategies to account for a multifaceted conceptualization of identity. Whichever perspective is taken and whatever method used, students' awareness of the *potential* implications of their responses can lead to altered choices, since they are not often privy to how researchers will interpret, alter, and represent student data (Harper, 2007).

The impact, then, of current enumeration strategies is that slight differences in the wording of the question, its format, or in the response options offered create presumably unanticipated variations in students' responses. Further, these variations are based on students' assumptions regarding how they *believe* they are supposed to respond and how their choices *might* be categorized and used. The implication for this personal, micro-level lack of information on the political, macro-level is that students might be self-identifying in ways that are not in line with or are not fully capturing their personal identity preferences or background. Further, since these students are not certain about how their responses are actually used or represented, their choices may not even result in the classification they had originally desired or anticipated. It seems that at the very least students should be privy to a discussion about how these questions and categories are interpreted and used. Institutional researchers and other questioning parties could supply more detailed notes at the time the survey or questionnaire is administered and to accompany any reported statistics. Students could decide whether to use this information when considering their response options.

Overall, there seem to be a number of opportunities for institutional research to better capture students and their intersecting identities. There are no clear strategies on how to best achieve this, and there are limitations to any approach, but I'd like to propose a few implications for institutional researchers to consider. The first is to track identity over the span of college rather than assume that identity is static. Relying on admissions data alone to capture identity omits the developmental changes that are expected among the college student population. A related recommendation is to compare students' responses to identity questions at multiple time points and then report these changes in order to better understand the complexity of longitudinal changes.

Third, related to intersectionality, is to offer cross-categorical comparisons (for example, rather than reporting results by race alone, combine race and gender). As discussed in this chapter, this does not fully capture the theoretical assumptions of intersectionality but might be an imperfect step toward a more complete view of students' identities. Another related recommendation is to allow the issue being examined at the time to help determine which cross-categorical analyses are most salient. For example, a financial aid analysis might include comparisons within and across race and class.

A fifth recommendation is to be transparent to survey participants about how questions of identity will be aggregated or recoded and then reported. College admissions applications are perhaps most suited for this since they are usually accompanied by a document detailing further explanation or instructions about specific questions. Another recommendation is to offer more opportunities for students to self-identify using their own words—for example, asking students to complete the sentence, "I am . . ." and then offering an outlet for that information to be reported. Finally, when asking students about their identity choices, it is important to discuss multiple contexts since their answers could be context-specific. Accounting for this complexity could reveal different responses that are specific to particular contexts, and it could explain the meaning students associate with those identity choices.

Conclusion

Capturing students' complex identities is a complicated endeavor that is highly sensitive to context and politics. In higher education, we use categories to classify individuals, foster comparison across groups, and research group differences across a vast number of outcomes. We do so with little attention to how we are capturing this information, and without knowing whether this information accurately describes students and how they conceptualize their own identity. College affords students the freedom to question their own identity and the independence to reconceptualize previous understandings of it. If our strategies to capture identity in research and practice serve also to inform and shape how students think about themselves and others, we need to question our strategies and the extent to which they reflect the true diversity of all college students. Capturing measures of identity is essential because of its deep integration into public discourse, policies, and practices; however, it is an imperfect, dynamic process. This discussion has revealed just how complicated it is and how limited our current static, unchanging, and one-dimensional approaches are. It is possible, however, that conceptualizations of identity can be improved by using a more fluid, dynamic, and multidimensional perspective.

References

Abes, E. S., Jones, S. R., and McEwen, M. K. "Reconceptualizing the Model of Multiple Dimensions of Identity: The Role of Meaning-Making Capacity in the Construction of Multiple Identities." *Journal of College Student Development,* 2007, 48(1), 1–22.

Bayer, A. "Construction of a Race Item for Survey Research." *Public Opinion Quarterly*, 1972–73, *36*, 592–602.

Bowleg, L. "When Black + Lesbian + Woman ≠ Black Lesbian Woman: The Methodological Challenges of Qualitative and Quantitative Intersectionality Research." *Sex Roles*, 2008, *59*, 312–325.

Cohen, P. C. *A Calculating People: The Spread of Numeracy in Early America*. Chicago: University of Chicago Press, 1982.

Cohen, P., Fink, G., Conley, V. M., and Sapp, M. *Implementing New IPEDS Race/Ethnicity Standards in Postsecondary Institutions*, AIR Webinar, September 17, 2008. Retrieved from http://www.airweb.org/page.asp?page=1503.

Creswell, J. W. *Research Design: Qualitative, Quantitative, and Mixed-Methods Approaches* (3rd ed.). Thousand Oaks, Calif.: Sage, 2009.

Cross, W. E., Jr. *Shades of Black: Diversity in African American Identity*. Philadelphia: Temple, 1991.

Diamond, L. M., and Butterworth, M. "Questioning Gender and Sexual Identity: Dynamic Links over Time." *Sex Roles*, 2008, *59*, 365–376.

Evans, N. J., Forney, D. S., Guido, F. M., Patton, L. D., and Renn, K. A. *Student Development in College: Theory, Research, and Practice*. San Francisco: Jossey-Bass, 2010.

"Final Guidance on Maintaining, Collecting, and Reporting Racial and Ethnic Data to the U.S. Department of Education." *Federal Register*, 72 (202), Oct. 19, 2007.

Harper, C. E. *Count Me In: A Mixed-Methods Analysis of the Theoretical, Methodological, and Practical Implications of Accounting for Multiracial Backgrounds in Higher Education*. Unpublished doctoral dissertation, University of California, Los Angeles, 2007.

Harris, D. R., and Sim, J. J. "Who Is Multiracial? Assessing the Complexity of Lived Race." *American Sociological Review*, 2002, *67*(4), 614–627.

Howard, R. D., and Borland, K. W., Jr. "Integrating Qualitative and Quantitative Information for Effective Institutional Research." In H. R. Borland Jr. (ed.), *Balancing Qualitative and Quantitative for Effective Decision-Making Support*. New Directions for Institutional Research, no. 112. San Francisco: Jossey-Bass, 2001.

Jones, S. R., and McEwen, M. K. "A Conceptual Model of Multiple Dimensions of Identity." *Journal of College Student Development*, 2000, *41*, 405–414.

Josselson, R. *Revising Herself: The Story of Women's Identity from College to Midlife*. New York: Oxford University Press, 1996.

McCall, L. "The Complexity of Intersectionality." *Signs: Journal of Women in Culture and Society*, 2005, *30*(3), 1771–1800.

Morning, A. "New Faces, Old Faces: Counting the Multiracial Population Past and Present." In H. DeBose and L. Winters (eds.), *New Faces in a Changing America: Multiracial Identity in the 21st Century*. Thousand Oaks, Calif.: Sage, 2002.

Nash, J. C. "Re-Thinking Intersectionality." *Feminist Review*, 2008, *89*, 1–15.

Padilla, A., and Kelley, M. *One Box Isn't Enough: An Analysis of How U.S. Colleges and Universities Classify Mixed Heritage Students*. Seattle: Mavin Foundation, 2005.

Perkins, M. L. "The Use of Quantitative and Qualitative Information in Institutional Decision Making." In H. R. Borland Jr. (ed.), *Balancing Qualitative and Quantitative for Effective Decision-Making Support*. New Directions for Institutional Research, no. 112. San Francisco: Jossey-Bass, 2001.

Renn, K. A., and Lunceford, C. J. "Because the Numbers Matter: Transforming Postsecondary Education Data on Student Race and Ethnicity to Meet the Challenges of a Changing Nation." *Educational Policy*, 2004, *18*(5), 752–783.

Reynolds, A. L., and Pope, R. L. "The Complexities of Diversity: Exploring Multiple Oppressions." *Journal of Counseling and Development*, 1991, *70*, 174–180.

Shields, S. A. "Gender: An Intersectionality Perspective." *Sex Roles*, 2008, 59, 301–311. DOI 10.1007/s11199-008-9501-8.

Stewart, D. L. "Researcher as Instrument: Understanding 'Shifting' Findings in Constructivist Research." *Journal of Student Affairs Research and Practice*, 2010, 47(3), 291–306.

CASANDRA E. HARPER is assistant professor of higher education in the educational leadership and policy analysis department at the University of Missouri.

INDEX

OTHER TITLES AVAILABLE IN THE
NEW DIRECTIONS FOR INSTITUTIONAL RESEARCH SERIES
Paul D. Umbach, Editor-in-Chief

IR 150   **Validity and Limitations of College Student Self-Report Data**
Serge Herzog, Nicholas A. Bowman
Higher education administrators, institutional researchers (IR), and scholars
rely heavily on the survey responses of college students, not least to meet
mounting accountability pressures to document student learning and
institutional effectiveness. However, research on the accuracy of students'
self-reported learning, development, and experiences is quite limited. To
address this critical issue, *Validity and Limitations of College Student Self-
Report Data* provides seven empirical studies that examine the validity, use,
and interpretation of such data, with an emphasis on student self-reported
gains. The chapters are written by leading scholars in the field of college
student self-reports, and they provide IR practitioners several analytical
frameworks to gauge the accuracy of student survey data. The cumulative
findings from this volume suggest that self-reported gains exhibit some
significant biases, and they often do not constitute an adequate proxy for
longitudinal measures of learning and development. Still, student self-
reports offer important subjective impressions about learning and affective
development that may complement direct measures of outcomes, together
yielding a more comprehensive picture of the college experience.
ISBN: 978-1-1181-3416-0

IR 149   **Assessing Complex General Education Student Learning Outcomes**
Jeremy D. Penn
One of the greatest challenges in assessing student learning in general
education programs is addressing the tension between selecting easy-
to-measure learning outcomes that have little value or bearing on our
institutions' goals and selecting meaningful and substantial learning
outcomes that are complex and difficult to assess. Many institutions that
have recently replaced their cafeteria-style general education programs
with general education programs that focus on complex student learning
outcomes find themselves at a loss in attempting to gather evidence on
student achievement of these outcomes for internal improvement and
external accountability purposes. This volume of *New Directions for
Institutional Research* makes a compelling case that institutions can and
should be assessing consequential, complex general education student
learning outcomes. It also gives faculty members and assessment leaders the
tools and resources to take ownership of this important work. Part One of
this volume provides an argument for why we should be assessing general
education and describes a framework, based on a rigorous psychological
research approach, for engaging in assessment. The six chapters in Part Two
show how this work can be (and is being) done for six important learning
outcomes: critical thinking, quantitative reasoning, teamwork, intercultural
competence, civic knowledge and engagement, and integrative learning.
The volume closes with recommendations on needed innovations in general
education assessment and presents a research agenda for future work.
ISBN: 978-1-1180-9133-3

IR 148   Students of Color in STEM
Shaun R. Harper, Christopher B. Newman
Why are some racial minorities so underrepresented as degree candidates in science, technology, engineering, and mathematics (STEM)? Why are they so underprepared for college-level math and science courses? Why are their grades and other achievement indicators disproportionately lower than their white counterparts? Why do so many of them change their majors to non-STEM fields? And why do so few pursue graduate degrees in STEM? These five questions are continuously recycled in the study of students of color in STEM. Offered in this volume of *New Directions for Institutional Research* are new research ideas and frameworks that have emerged from recent studies of minorities in STEM fields across a wide array of institution types: large research universities, community colleges, minority-serving institutions, and others. The chapter authors counterbalance examinations of student underperformance and racial disparities in STEM with insights into the study of factors that enable minority student success.
ISBN: 978-1-1180-1402-8

IR 147   System Offices for Community College Institutional Research
Willard C. Hom
This volume of *New Directions for Institutional Research* examines a professional niche that tends to operate with a low profile while playing a major role in state policies—the system office for community college institutional research. As states, regions, and the federal government seek ways to evaluate and improve the performance of community colleges, this office has grown in importance. The chapter authors, all institutional researchers in this area, draw a timely state-of-the-niche portrait by showing how this office varies across states, how it varies from other institutional research offices within states, and the implications its history and prospects have for the future. This volume will be particularly useful for those who deal with higher education policy at the state, regional, or federal level; on-campus institutional researchers; and individuals who currently work in or with these system offices.
ISBN: 978-04709-39543

IR 146   Institutional Research and Homeland Security
Nicolas A. Valcik
Although homeland security has captured the public's attention in recent years, higher education institutions have had to contend with emergency situations and security issues long before 9/11 occurred. Well known incidents such as the Unabomber attacks and decades of sporadic school shootings brought violence to college campuses long before the Department of Homeland Security was established. Despite these past security issues and the passage of the PATRIOT Act, very little research has been performed on homeland security issues and higher education institutions. This volume of *New Directions for Institutional Research* examines how new federal regulations impact institutional research and higher education institutions. This volume also addresses key issues such as right-to-privacy regulations, criminal background checks, the Student and Exchange Visitor Information System (SEVIS), information technology security, the use of geographic information systems as a research tool, hazardous materials (HAZMAT) management, and the impact of natural disasters and manmade threats on applications and enrollment.
ISBN: 978-04709-03148

IR 145   **Diversity and Educational Benefits**
Serge Herzog
Campus climate studies and research on the impact of diversity in higher
education abound. On closer examination, however, the corpus of findings
on the role of diversity and how diversity is captured with campus climate
surveys reveals both conceptual and methodological limitations. This
volume of *New Directions for Institutional Research* addresses these limitations
with the inclusion of studies by institutional research (IR) practitioners
who make use of data that furnish new insights into the relationships
among student diversity, student perception of campus climate, and student
sociodemographic background—and how those relationships affect academic
outcomes. Each chapter emphasizes how IR practitioners benefit from the
conceptual and analytical approach laid out, and each chapter provides a
framework to gauge the contribution of diversity to educational benefits.
The findings revealed in this volume cast doubt on the benefits of student
diversity purported in previous research. At a minimum, the influence of
student diversity is neither linear nor unidirectional, but operates within a
complex web of interrelated factors that shape the student experience.
ISBN: 978-04707-67276

IR 144   **Data-Driven Decision Making in Intercollegiate Athletics**
Jennifer Lee Hoffman, James Soto Antony, Daisy D. Alfaro
Data related to intercollegiate athletics are often a small part of campus
financial and academic data reporting, but they generate significant interest
at any institution that sponsors varsity sports. The demands for documen-
tation, accountability, and data-driven decision making related to college
athletics have grown increasingly sophisticated. These demands come
from the press, campus decision makers, researchers, state and federal
agencies, the National Collegiate Athletic Association, and the public.
Despite the growth of data sources and the ease of access that information
technology affords, gaps still exist between what we think we know about
college athletics and supporting data. The challenge for institutional
researchers is to continue developing consistent data sources that inform the
policy and governance of college athletics. This volume of *New Directions
for Institutional Research* introduces the reader to the primary and secondary
sources of data on college athletics and their utility for decision making. The
authors describe the existing landscape of data about student athletes and
intercollegiate athletics and the measures that are still needed.
ISBN: 978-04706-08289

IR 143   **Imagining the Future of Institutional Research**
Christina Leimer
With the increasing demands placed on colleges and universities—requirements for continuous improvement, evidence-based decision making, and
accountability—institutional research offices must do more than report
and fill data requests. In the context of shrinking budgets, institutions must
search for more efficient and effective ways of working, make decisions about
which work will continue to be performed and how, and perhaps reorganize
their existing programs, structures, and patterns. This too may demand more
of institutional research. A decade ago, M. W. Peterson pro-posed in volume
104 of *New Directions for Institutional Research* that the future challenge for
institutional research would be not only to help institu-tions improve but
to help facilitate their redesign and transformation. It appears that time has
arrived. At most institutions, however, for institutional research to play
such a substantive role, the field will need to redesign and transform itself.
In this volume, the editor and authors take a proactive, strategic stance by
imagining the future of institutional research and how to achieve it.
ISBN: 978-04705-69269

NEW DIRECTIONS FOR INSTITUTIONAL RESEARCH
ORDER FORM SUBSCRIPTION AND SINGLE ISSUES

DISCOUNTED BACK ISSUES:

Use this form to receive 20% off all back issues of *New Directions for Institutional Research*.
All single issues priced at **$23.20** (normally $29.00)

TITLE	ISSUE NO.	ISBN
_____	_____	_____
_____	_____	_____
_____	_____	_____

Call 888-378-2537 or see mailing instructions below. When calling, mention the promotional code JBNND
to receive your discount. For a complete list of issues, please visit www.josseybass.com/go/ndir

SUBSCRIPTIONS: (1 YEAR, 4 ISSUES)

☐ New Order   ☐ Renewal

U.S.	☐ Individual: $100	☐ Institutional: $280
CANADA/MEXICO	☐ Individual: $100	☐ Institutional: $320
ALL OTHERS	☐ Individual: $124	☐ Institutional: $354

Call 888-378-2537 or see mailing and pricing instructions below.
Online subscriptions are available at www.onlinelibrary.wiley.com

ORDER TOTALS:

Issue / Subscription Amount: $ _____

Shipping Amount: $ _____
(for single issues only – subscription prices include shipping)

Total Amount: $ _____

SHIPPING CHARGES:	
First Item	$5.00
Each Add'l Item	$3.00

(No sales tax for U.S. subscriptions. Canadian residents, add GST for subscription orders. Individual rate subscriptions must
be paid by personal check or credit card. Individual rate subscriptions may not be resold as library copies.)

BILLING & SHIPPING INFORMATION:

☐ **PAYMENT ENCLOSED:** *(U.S. check or money order only. All payments must be in U.S. dollars.)*

☐ **CREDIT CARD:** ☐ VISA ☐ MC ☐ AMEX

Card number _____ Exp. Date _____

Card Holder Name _____ Card Issue # _____

Signature _____ Day Phone _____

☐ **BILL ME:** *(U.S. institutional orders only. Purchase order required.)*

Purchase order # _____
Federal Tax ID 13559302 • GST 89102-8052

Name _____

Address _____

Phone _____ E-mail _____

Copy or detach page and send to: **John Wiley & Sons, PTSC, 5th Floor**
989 Market Street, San Francisco, CA 94103-1741

Order Form can also be faxed to: **888-481-2665**

PROMO JBNND